AN ELECTRONIC
CASH AND CREDIT
SYSTEM

AUTHORS

Allan H. Anderson

Donald T. Cannell

Terrance A. Gibbons

G. Peter Grote

John Henn

J. Bradley Kennedy

Michael B. Muir

Norman D. Potter

Robert H. Whitby

AN ELECTRONIC CASH AND CREDIT SYSTEM

AMERICAN MANAGEMENT ASSOCIATION
NEW YORK

The softbound edition of this book has been distributed without charge to AMA members enrolled in the Finance Division. Those members who are enrolled in other divisions, or who wish extra copies, may order the book in a hardbound edition at $5.00 per copy. Price to nonmembers, $7.50.

This book was originally prepared as a research report in partial fulfillment of the requirements of Professor Georges F. Doriot's Manufacturing Course at the Harvard University Graduate School of Business Administration during the academic year 1965-1966. The conclusions and opinions expressed herein are those of the authors and do not necessarily represent the views of the Harvard Business School, Professor Doriot, or individuals, business firms, associates, or government agencies contacted.

Library of Congress catalog card number: 66-27016.

TO

PROFESSOR GEORGES F. DORIOT

Teacher and Inspiration

this book is gratefully dedicated

FOREWORD

THE AUTHORS formally established themselves as a research and consulting group to fulfill the requirements of Professor Georges F. Doriot's Manufacturing Course at the Harvard Business School. This book is the result of a report prepared to "make a contribution to the future of American business," as required by Professor Doriot. Original research and writing were conducted over a period of seven months. The methods used to gather information included interviews with many individuals who have pioneered in this system concept, a mail questionnaire, field trips to numerous institutions and companies, and an extensive search of relevant literature, including manufacturers' and consultants' brochures. A formal presentation of this system in which the authors participated was given in Boston at the 1966 Spring Joint Computer Conference.

We express grateful thanks to Professor Georges F. Doriot, who challenged us to reach beyond the limits of our conventional expectations; to Mr. Dale L. Reistad of the American Bankers Association for his invaluable assistance and guidance to our research effort; to Mr. Richard E. Sprague, partner of the accounting firm of Touche, Ross, Bailey & Smart, for his insight into previous research on this topic; to Mr. Donald R. Schnee, vice president, and Mr. Walter G. Trabbold, comptroller, of the Bank of Delaware, for permitting us to visit their pilot system; and to Booz, Allen and Hamilton, Inc., First National City Bank, and Sperry Utah, which supplied us with invaluable research assistance. Many other individuals took time from busy routines to respond to the questionnaire, to submit to interviews, or to assist in preparation of our manuscript. Their contributions to our work were significant, and it is with regret that we can only thank them collectively.

We hope our observations and projections provide a sound basis for understanding the potential of this system and will provoke creative thought in wrestling with the many problems which will emerge in adopting this system.

THE AUTHORS

PREFACE

Practical applications of on-line real-time computer systems are causing the emergence of an economy no longer dependent on the flow of checks and currency for its livelihood.

The communities of banking, retail merchandising, and consumer credit are beginning to use these systems for problems of credit inquiry, credit accumulation, and electronic transfer of demand deposit balances. The evolution of systems networks, linking banks, stores, and credit bureaus with one another poses tremendous problems and opportunities for those whose professions and organizations will be affected by this integration.

This study is written primarily as an aid for those planning and operating executives of the banking, credit, and merchandising communities whose responsible positions require that they be fully aware of the emerging trends and technologies which are so rapidly changing the nature of their businesses. The study should also be of value to the hardware manufacturers, systems engineers, and communications experts who must continue to provide the technological requirements of the future's "checkless-cashless society."

CONTENTS

EXHIBITS

CHAPTER I

AN OVERVIEW •

Though speculations about developments in the future are sometimes unrealistic, it now appears certain that by 1980 very few American shoppers will be carrying bulky checkbooks in their purses or large amounts of cash in their wallets. The present proliferation of credit cards of all sizes, shapes, and colors will also be largely a thing of the past. Money will still serve as a unit of accounts, a standard of value, and a store of wealth. However, money as we know it today (in terms of cash and checks and a variety of credit card charge accounts) will take on a new appearance when used as a medium of exchange involving most consumer transactions. The story of this change in money and credit transfer mechanisms is the subject of this book.

Instead of paying for groceries at the supermarket check-out counter by cash (acquired by cashing a check at her bank or elsewhere), the housewife of the future will simply hand the store clerk a unique "funds identification card" which she alone can use. The clerk, before ringing up the amount of her purchase, will insert this identification card into an electronic apparatus which "reads" the card and establishes immediately and automatically an electronic communication to the customer's bank account. If sufficient funds are held in her account to cover this transaction or if the customer has an established line of credit with her bank large enough to cover the transaction, an indicator on the card-reading apparatus will inform the clerk accordingly. The clerk will then activate the device, causing the amount of the purchase to be automatically deducted from the customer's account and added to the account of the supermarket. This simple, foolproof feat might then be repeated a few minutes later by the same housewife in a neighboring department store as she pays for a dress that she has selected. The department store clerk will, in a similar manner, insert the customer's machine-readable "identification card" into a "terminal device," repeating the process described above; only, this time, the department store will be credited with the amount of the purchase. If, on the way home, this same housewife buys gasoline for her car, she will pay the service station attendant by handing him her card and initiating yet another automated transaction. Assume she arrives home and discovers in the mail a request for some extra pocket money from her son in college in another city. If she is softhearted, she will simply key in the account number of her son's bank account on her own "touch-tone telephone," insert her card into a special receptacle on the telephone, and punch in the amount she is willing to part with on her telephone keys—transferring demand deposit funds electronically, instantaneously, and by telephone.

The transactions just described will be repeated several times daily by most American consumers all over the country. Terminal devices designed to receive funds identification cards will be found in most stores and in most service outlets. Touch-tone telephones with the optional bank-by-phone feature will be universally available. Several hundred million transactions of the type described will be made daily, facilitating greater economy, security, and convenience than are presently realized today through the use of cash, checks, and proliferation of credit cards. The complete automation of the funds transfer system will mean the adoption of a whole new philosophy of money and monetary exchange. This new concept has been christened by many the "checkless" or the "cashless" society.

The emergence of a checkless society appears imminent, as we shall show, with only a few developments necessary before such a system will be operational. Most of these developments will require only a refining of present knowledge. No major technological or economical breakthroughs are foreseen which will have to precede the successful evolution of such a system.

In brief, four basic technical requirements will be needed to execute electronic funds transfers in the checkless society. First, small, inexpensive, and reliable terminal devices must be located at the point of purchase or site of transaction. Second, massive random-access computer files (containing information, for example, on individuals' current deposit balances, credit information, or both) must be operational. Third, there must be a fast and efficient communications network linking terminal devices with central data files. The use of a central switching computer for linking systems participants will be necessary to facilitate the proper flow of information throughout these networks. Fourth, as mentioned previously, a machine-readable, unique, identification card for each individual will be required to activate the transaction system. A detailed and more precise clarification of the system we envision, and of its components, will be presented in Chapter II.

Before turning to such details, however, it seems appropriate that the checkless society be placed in perspective. It should already be evident to the reader that the described system signifies the greatest innovation in the history and evolution of money in this century. Reflection on the past, however, shows that other major innovations, with similarly far-reaching consequences, have occurred on numerous occasions.

The original barter system, for example, evolved several thousand years ago when primitive man realized that to satisfy his personal need for goods and commodities, trade with his neighbor was worthwhile and necessary. However, as man further developed and his societies became more sophisticated, his economic needs became more diverse and complex. The barter system was often cumbersome. The trader really needed some sort of common medium of exchange, something that was easy to carry, scarce, divisible into units, acceptable to all tastes within society, and, finally, applicable for use in different types of trade. This need was soon satisfied by the innovation of a medium of exchange that was recognized by all as being symbolic of value. Gold and other rare metals that could be stamped into coins of standard weight soon began to serve these functions. As international trade expanded, even the fair exchange of rare metals and coins became an acute problem. International merchants must have spent endless hours figuring the value of their various stores. In the more complex and specialized society that finally evolved, the need for a better value exchange mechanism was satisfied by a new innovation—banks. Alert middlemen came to expand their money services to include real banking operations whereby clients of these "bankers" simply deposited their coin and gold for safekeeping. In return, written receipts were issued to the clients. Since these receipts symbolized value and since society needed a medium of exchange that was less awkward than heavy coin, another innovation in the evolution of money occurred—the use of paper as a medium of exchange. Then, of course, came the check and the banking system we know today.

Now, with over 60 million checks being written each day in America, the need for reducing the growing time and expense in handling this paper is a stark reality. It is the authors' contention that by 1985 (when the number of checks processed daily would otherwise have exceeded 100 million) the check will have become as obsolete as the barter system and that a universal "funds identification card" will have become the new, if not the ultimate medium of value exchange.

We do not consider this contention to be idle speculation. The purpose of this book is to show the how's, when's, where's, and why's of the value exchange system we can expect to be using by the 1980's. Chapter II presents, from a functional point of view, a detailed description of the electronic system configuration we envision for replacing most checks, currencies, and credit cards. Chapter III delves into some of the particular technical problems relating to the system we propose, with detailed examination of some of the specific hardware, software, and peripheral equipment requirements for constructing an automated transfer system.

In Chapter IV we will discuss the banking sector of our economy, in terms of both how it operates today and how close many banks are to implementing the concepts and innovations we propose. In Chapters V and VI a similar analysis of both the credit sector and the retailing sector is presented, again with the specific intention of showing the reader the dislocations and costs, and the opportunities and benefits, which electronic funds systems imply for each of these sectors. Chapter VII relates some of the implications this system will have and is having in the international sphere. Chapter VIII provides a brief discussion of some of the legal, social, political, and economic problems and implications we can expect to accompany this evolution in the funds exchange process. To conclude, the authors provide in Chapter IX a brief timetable for action. Some of the next steps which future systems participants should be taking to facilitate a rapid and successful development of a checkless society are presented.

CHAPTER II

WHAT IS AN ELECTRONIC
CASH AND CREDIT SYSTEM? •

I T IS THE CONTENTION of the authors that most cash and credit transactions
of the future will be conducted through on-line, real-time (OLRT) computer systems. What is meant by OLRT, what this "electronic cash and
credit system" will look like, and how it will operate are discussed in this
chapter.

ON-LINE, REAL-TIME

Let us turn first to the on-line part of the concept. By this term we mean
a computer system with a configuration specifically designed to allow direct
communication between a number of remote input-output devices and a
central information file. To this extent today's telephone system could be
considered a kind of on-line system: By the use of remote devices, a party
can communicate with other devices which are also on-line to the system
through a central switching mechanism.

To further our understanding of "on-line," let us consider, by way of
contrast, a typical "off-line" system. The strictly in-house telephonic networks used in some apartment buildings for security protection are good
examples. The users of these off-line systems cannot communicate with
other apartment buildings, other cities, or any other points not in-house.
Similarly, an off-line computer system is one which is operated independently from other computer systems and which is self-contained. It is not
designed to receive data directly relayed from other computers or to dispatch data directly to other computers or input-output devices.

To help explain the real-time part of the OLRT concept, we will draw another analogy to the telephone system. The process of dialing and obtaining a connection on a usual phone call may take from 5 to 15 seconds, depending on the magnitude of the digits and the number of switching circuits involved. One establishes a communications link in a "reasonable" period of time. Once engaged, conversation can be transmitted from the sending unit, over a communications link, and to a receiving device seemingly instantaneously. Replies, in turn, can be sent back via the communications link "instantaneously," as though no perceived passage of time had taken place for this communications process. Clearly, were a telephone user required to wait for an hour (or even a minute) prior to establishing communications linkage, he might not be satisfied with the service. Similarly, one would be dissatisfied with telephones if there were even a few seconds delay between transmission of conversation and reception of reply. Telephonic real-time means transmission rates so rapid that delays are imperceptible to the users.

The concept of real-time is really nothing more than a kind of tolerance limit on the delay experienced between the transmission of a message and the receipt of a response, between a query and an answer. The tolerance limit in humans can be measured perhaps in terms of a few seconds; between two computers the limit may be scaled down to thousandths or millionths of a second. Our working definition of "real-time" in the electronic cash and credit system will be that amount of time in which a human can communicate, for information or transaction purposes, with a central computer and receive an answer without exceeding "reasonable" or "tolerable" amounts of elapsed time.

As a first requirement then, the proposed OLRT electronic cash and credit system will, by definition, be capable of permitting access from remote locations to a central computer file and will be capable of communicating and receiving answers within a time period so short that the communications process will be perceived by the systems users as taking place instantaneously.

Let us now discuss in detail a proposed configuration for such a funds transfer network. This presentation will be largely functional in nature, describing with the aid of flow charts the proposed OLRT concept and explaining how each of the various on-line participants in the system fits in. These on-line participants will be discussed in the following order: retailers, banks, credit information bureaus and credit grantors, home users, industrial organizations, government agencies, and those providing auxiliary services. The more detailed and technical aspects of the system (such as hardware requirements and the like) for each systems participant will be discussed in subsequent chapters; what immediately follows will be strictly a descriptive and functional discussion of each of the participants on-line to the system, including our view of the integrated relationships linking these participants.

ON-LINE RETAILERS

Discussion of the retailer participants of the system will be divided into three parts. First, there will be a description of equipment necessary to conduct OLRT cash and credit transactions. This is followed by an illustration of an actual OLRT cash transaction. Finally, we present a proposal as to how various types of retail organizations will fit into the OLRT funds transfer concept.

EQUIPMENT REQUIRED

Several basic equipment requirements are necessary to conduct an OLRT cash transaction from a retail outlet. First, there must be a remote terminal device or "black box" at the point of purchase which is capable of:

1. Initially identifying the customer from his unique identification card.
2. Verifying that the customer's account has sufficient funds to cover the transaction.
3. Verifying that the customer has properly identified himself (insuring that he is not fraudulantly using another person's card).
4. Entering the transaction into the system (communicating with both the customer's and the retailer's accounts at remote bank locations and activating an instantaneous transfer of demand deposit balances).

To turn first to the identification function, the customer would establish his initial identification to the system with an encoded identification card. Similar to one of today's credit cards, this card could be printed or hole-punched in such a manner that the terminal device could "read" the card and ascertain the number of the customer's checking account and the electronic address of this account. A hole-punched card is only one of several potential means of establishing initial identification. Other devices or identification systems may be utilized, as will be discussed in a subsequent treatment of the identification problem. The basic requirements for account number entry are about the same regardless of the kind of personal identification device used. Whatever the system, the corresponding terminal device must be capable of sensing and entering the identification information instantaneously and automatically from the customer's card.

In addition to initial identification, the added capability of verifying customer identification will probably be a requirement for the terminal devices. The necessity for verifying whether the customer possesses sufficient funds in his bank account to cover the amount of the transaction is obvious. The terminal must be designed to query automatically and instantaneously the account at the customer's bank, with the bank's computer then indicating to the clerk whether the account can accommodate the transaction. The answer transmitted to the retailer's terminal device need not indicate the total amount of funds available but may simply indicate a "yes" or "no" to govern completion of the proposed transaction.

Verification of customer identification might be required in some cases to make certain that the customer presenting an identifying instrument (for example, hole-punched card) to the terminal device is the same person who rightfully owns the card and whose account is stored in the bank's on-line account file. This type of verifying identification would seek to match for comparison a facsimile of the customer taken at point of purchase (such as a special descriptive characteristic of the customer) with a similar descriptive characteristic stored in the bank's on-line computer files or encoded in machine-readable form on the card itself. Sophisticated techniques of computer-aided identification verification will be dealt with later.

In order to possess the ability to identify and verify the customer and his ability to pay, the terminal device must be connected electronically with an OLRT communication system which has computer files at other remote locations containing certain customer information. These large computerized central files have recorded, among other things, the customer's demand deposit balance, as well as the retail store's balance. The terminal device, having automatically read the customer's account number on the identifying card, automatically generates a signal which locates the appropriate demand deposit account file for the customer. The terminal device also generates an automatic signal identifying the source of the input, in this case the coded name of the retail store. The appropriate demand deposit account file for the retail store is located automatically by the system. Once both account files are located, the terminal device, activated through the pressing of keys similar to those on a cash register (or a touch-tone telephone), signals the money amounts to be transacted. These signals proceed to the account files, deposit balances are charged as indicated, and the transaction is completed.

A retail purchase example. Having functionally described the requirements of the retail terminal device and the basic requirements of the communication system, let us now follow a typical transaction in the system.

For example, a housewife is about to pay for her week's groceries at the supermarket check-out counter. Referring to Exhibit 1, assume the housewife's checking account to be in Bank 1 while the supermarket maintains its account in Bank 2. Instead of paying for the groceries with cash or check, the housewife hands the check-out clerk her identification card. The clerk places the card in the terminal, and the terminal establishes communication with Bank 1's computer. This is shown by the heavy line in Exhibit 1. The communication link from the store to the bank is instantaneously established by a central switching computer which is simply a message router. As the clerk keys in the amount of the groceries, the computer at Bank 1 accesses the customer's demand deposit account as stored in computer memory and verifies the ability of the account to perform the transaction. When notification of sufficient funds is complete, activation of the terminal device initiates an automatic transfer of the funds from the customer's account in Bank 1 to the supermarket's account in Bank 2. This transfer is graphically illustrated by the dotted lines in Exhibit 1. The computer at Bank 2 notifies the terminal in the supermarket when the transfer is complete. Such a notification might also activate the automatic printing of a receipt for the housewife by the terminal device.

It must be re-emphasized that on-line identification, funds verification, and transfer of funds between the customer and the supermarket occurred in real-time. The entire process would have taken considerably less time than writing out a personal check and handing it to the check-out clerk. This process should be completed in no more than 10-15 seconds.

Configuration of input/output system. Beginning with this simple discussion of the terminal requirements, supported by illustration of a typical "instant" transaction of funds, the configuration for the retail sector in an electronic cash and credit system begins to take form. The next step is to realize that the retail on-line participants will include an entire spectrum of store types. There will be a few large, high-volume stores, such as the big department and appliance stores in big cities, many medium-volume large supermarkets, and an unlimited number of small outlets, such as corner shoe stores or liquor stores. Terminals, transmission requirements, and techniques will necessarily vary greatly to accommodate the varying volumes of transactions and the unique needs of the system participants.

Large stores such as Filene's in Boston or Macy's in New York might

ILLUSTRATION OF A RETAIL CASH TRANSACTION

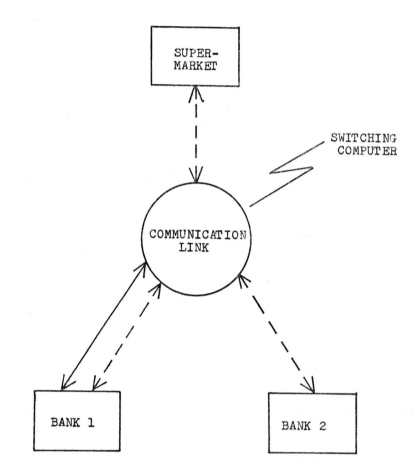

EXHIBIT 1

CONFIGURATION OF INPUT/OUTPUT SYSTEMS

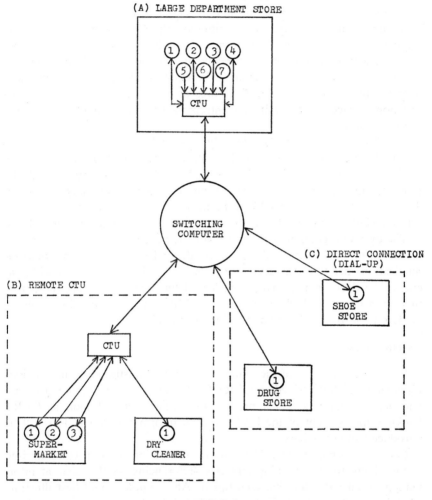

EXHIBIT 2

have a configuration similar to that shown in Exhibit 2. This diagram shows just one large department, with seven terminals connected to a central transmission unit (CTU). The CTU collects data transmissions from the terminals, batches them for transmission economies, and routes them at an efficient transmission density to the switching computer. The seven terminals would be located at various sales areas in the store. As Part (A) of Exhibit 2 shows, the CTU for each large department would be physically located within the department store. For those stores without the volume of transactions demanding an in-house CTU, a structure such as Part (B) of Exhibit 2 might apply. In this situation the CTU is not on the same physical premises as that of the terminals. Rather, the CTU is at a remote location, with several different stores connected for economic transmission to the central switching computer. This remote CTU might be owned and operated by a joint venture of the stores or could be maintained as a subscription service provided by an entrepreneurial concern other than the connected stores.

For those types of outlets with only small volumes of transactions, such as small shoe stores or corner drug stores, the communication network might be as shown in Part (C) of Exhibit 2. In this arrangement the terminals in the store are directly connected to the switching computer. This connection would not likely be an open circuit but would probably utilize a slight-delay telephone dial-up system using regular telephone lines.

The optimum communications network required to service a given configuration of retail stores will ultimately depend upon the volume of communications per terminal device and per store which the system will generate. The decision regarding open leased lines versus dial-up lines, multiple lines versus multichanneled, buffered lines, and so on, will simply be made on the basis of communications economics.

ON-LINE BANKS

Part of the structure of the banking sector was illustrated in the previous discussion which described an OLRT funds transaction between a customer and her supermarket. As a prelude to a more detailed look at OLRT banking, the concept of the bank's central information file (CIF) will be introduced and explained.

Central information file. The central information file is a computerized storage bank for maintaining and cross-referencing all the account information on an individual bank customer. An example would best illustrate what is meant by the CIF. Suppose that John Doe, married, is a bank customer and maintains the following accounts:
- Personal checking account for business reasons.
- Joint checking account with his wife.
- Joint savings account (wife).
- Personal trust account.
- Several savings accounts held jointly with his children.

- Mortgage account on his house.
- An installment loan account.

Now assume that all of these accounts are numbered and stored in a computer memory by account number and current balance. In another part of memory the name John Doe is stored along with a list of the numbers of each account. Finally, the individual accounts are coded so that they refer back to the master list. Thus, by the use of codes, the bank can access any or all of the accounts associated with John Doe, either by accessing one type of account and referring back to the master list, or by querying the master list directly. Knowledge of one account number or the customer's name enables the bank to determine instantly the status of all his accounts.

Strictly from an internal information viewpoint, the value of the CIF for the banking community can easily be recognized. In addition, however, the CIF concept has significant import for the proposed electronic cash and credit system. First of all, OLRT transactions require that all demand deposit accounts be stored and available to computerized random access. The CIF, if properly designed, can accommodate OLRT access, both for information inquiries and for transaction purposes. Thinking back to the description of the OLRT funds transaction, we recall the necessity that a CIF exist for the demand deposit accounts of both Bank 1 and Bank 2 is obvious. The very nature of the OLRT funds transfer concept requires instant access to bank account balances, possible only through computerized random access CIF's. Aspects of the identification-verification process also require special CIF capability. (The requirements of the CIF for accommodating credit transactions are also another part of the CIF story and will be discussed subsequently.)

Audit trail. An important aspect of the OLRT system of cash and credit transactions falling within the commercial banks' realm of operations is generation of an audit trail or "hard copy" record of the transactions handled by the system. This necessary audit trail would be automatically produced by recording on a magnetic tape record all transactions handled through each bank's computer. This tape could then be processed at night or during slack time to provide hard copy printouts on paper of all the transactions processed through the system, by account, by timeslice, or by any other desirable breakdown.

The purposes of making a transactions tape or audit trail are threefold. First, the printout from the tape might be used to check for any errors in entry or computation. Second, the tape or printout might be used to reconstruct any accounts or transactions destroyed because of a malfunction in the computer. Third, the tape records could be used to update the master account histories and thereby be used to produce the monthly accounting statements sent to customers.

Bank configuration. The cost of computers and associated memory storage for this type of OLRT system could restrict ownership of OLRT to only the larger banks. However, similar to the different communication linkups described in the retail sector, several alternatives are open to banks which cannot afford their own computers.

Exhibit 3 graphically illustrates some potential alternatives. Part (A) shows the large bank with its own computer and CIF. Part (B) describes a joint venture whereby Banks 1, 2, and 3 jointly own a single random-access CIF and have segregated the memory for the use of each bank. This arrangement could be financed and owned jointly by the banks or could be set up as a service bureau arrangement by an entrepreneur outside of the banking system. In the arrangement in Part (B), Banks 1, 2, and 3 would have input/output terminals enabling them to communicate with their own accounts. Part (C) illustrates a correspondent bank relationship which is similar to Part (B), except that Bank 1 would have the computer on its own premises and Bank 2 would own accounts in a section of the memory. Other types of arrangements are possible, but we believe that these three include the most likely combinations.

There are, at present, certain legal constraints which limit joint bank ownerships and even limit the amount of computer hardware a bank may own for its own use. The first section of Chapter VIII discusses some of these legal problems, the general implication being that such laws can be changed to meet the requirements of the proposed system.

The ownership and sharing of the central switching computer, which routes data through the system and serves all the system participants, is yet another question. Part of Chapter VIII deals with this problem in more detail. However, since the switching computer is essentially a telecommunications expediter, it is really an integral part of only the communications system itself. Just as central switching devices control and route message flow through today's telephonic networks (in a rather unnoticed and inconspicuous way) so will the central switching computer(s) be integral with the communications system employed for electronic funds transfer.

ON-LINE CREDIT INFORMATION BUREAUS AND CREDIT GRANTORS

The example cited earlier of an OLRT supermarket purchase was presented as a cash transaction; that is, as a moving of demand deposit funds from one account to another. Let us now discuss a related form of funds

ALTERNATE BANK CONFIGURATIONS

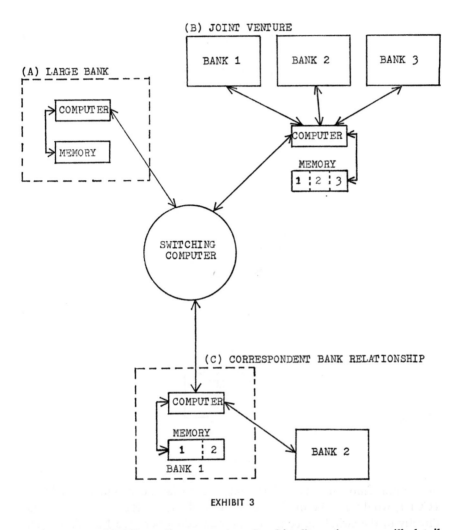

EXHIBIT 3

exchange, an OLRT credit transaction. In this discussion, we will detail how the system will assist in the evaluation of a customer's credit worthiness and also suggest some of the institutional sources of credit that can be put on-line to the present system.

The computer credit file. The reader is asked to consider a computerized information file, existing within the proposed market area and containing historical credit information on each individual living within the area. This

OLRT CONNECTION OF THE COMPUTER CREDIT FILE

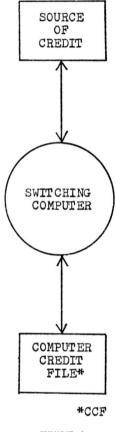

*CCF

EXHIBIT 4

huge information file, henceforth referred to as the computer credit file (CCF), would also be on-line to the rest of the OLRT network and tied directly to the switching computer introduced earlier (see Exhibit 4). The credit source shown in Exhibit 4 will be assumed to be a bank for purposes of this illustration.

Line-of-credit overdraft. Now assume John Doe, a customer of the bank, anticipates the need to make purchases which he cannot or does not wish to transact with the amount of funds in his demand deposit account. Mr. Doe will approach his bank to negotiate a special bank line-of-credit. The bank will allow Mr. Doe to overdraw his demand deposit account up to a certain amount, depending on Doe's credit worthiness, his relationship with the bank, and so on. Such a line-of-credit would not become an interest-bearing loan for Mr. Doe until his demand deposit account became "overdrawn," at which time the loan would become automatic in the amount of Doe's overdraft.

CCF inquiry. The bank, already tied into the system, could take action on Doe's request for a line-of-credit immediately. The loan officer would simply request, through a special kind of terminal device on-line to the network, that the credit information on Doe stored in the system's CCF be made available. The CCF would be designed to produce a standard block of information for this type of credit inquiry and could then transmit Doe's credit history to the bank over the electronic network. Thus the loan officer at the bank would be able to obtain a credit history on Doe while Doe is still at the officer's desk in the bank. On the basis of this information, the bank officer can decide a proper amount of credit to extend to Doe.

Computerized credit analysis. An added feature, quite feasible with the computer technology now available, would allow the loan officer to request the CCF to perform an instant credit analysis and rating of Doe's credit worthiness, rather than simply requesting the CCF to provide historical information about Doe. Through a computerized scoring process, the information in the CCF would be automatically evaluated and scored, the loan officer receiving either the scored credit worthiness of Doe or even a computerized reply recommending specific action. (A later chapter will discuss OLRT credit information services and credit evaluation in more detail.) Once the bank officer establishes the amount of the line-of-credit to be offered Doe, Doe's demand deposit account can be quickly modified within the bank's own CIF to permit OLRT overdraft payments up to Doe's maximum line-of-credit; and Mr. Doe can begin generating credit transactions within the system. Of course, Mr. Doe will have to pay an interest service charge to the bank on the basis of the amount of credit he uses and the length of time he is in a credit position.

A credit transaction example. Now John Doe is able to buy that washing machine. He enters a department store, chooses a model, and hands the clerk his identification card. The clerk places the card into the terminal which accesses Doe's account in Bank 1 and transfers funds to pay for the washing machine to Bank 2, where the department store has its account (see Exhibit 5). Since the purchase amount exceeds the amount of funds in Doe's demand deposit account, the line-of-credit programmed into his

ILLUSTRATION OF A CREDIT TRANSACTION

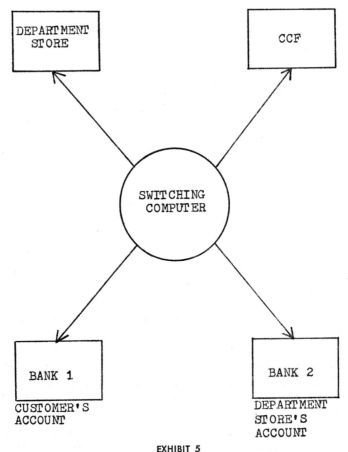

EXHIBIT 5

account absorbs the credit need and provides the funds for transfer to Bank 2. This overdraft remains outstanding, of course, until Doe's account receives an inflow of funds. Periodically, Doe's account will be debited with appropriate interest and principal charges to cover the credit extension.

Ancillary credit input. Let us briefly consider the case where Doe's bank will not give him the needed credit or where Doe chooses for some personal reason not to go to his bank for the credit. In this case, he can turn to one of many regular ancillary loan institutions, such as a savings and loan institution, a credit union, or even a high-interest, high-risk lender. Since

TIE-IN OF ANCILLARY CREDIT INSTITUTION

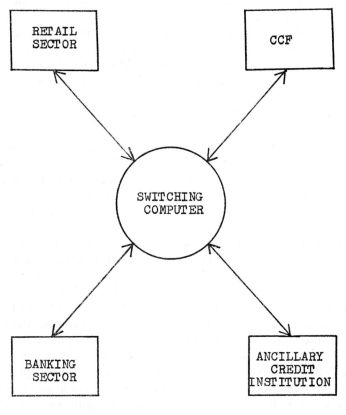

EXHIBIT 6

these kinds of institutions would also be on-line, Doe could simply negotiate a loan with one of them, the institution then transferring the loaned
funds (through the OLRT system) into Doe's demand deposit account
(see Exhibit 6). Repayments could be preauthorized by Doe to take place
each month. A principal payment, interest payment, or both, could automatically be transferred from Doe's account to the loaning institution each
month, each pay day, or however Doe would specify.

It is entirely likely that retail stores might choose to retain their customer
credit services themselves in spite of OLRT credit availability to the customer from external sources. In this case, the retail store could still utilize

the CCF for credit information in the same way as did the bank or as the savings-and-loan lender might have done. The availability of OLRT credit information and credit analysis from the CCF would enable the store to make a credit check at the time of purchase and to extend store credit to Doe if he meets the store's standards. The retail store in the system now has the alternatives of extending store credit on a purchase-by-purchase basis or perhaps on a revolving credit arrangement, depending on the OLRT credit check from the CCF. In either case, Doe can liquidate his store debt by preauthorizing his bank to make monthly payments to the store on an automatic basis discussed earlier.

Whether OLRT credit is offered by the banks, the ancillary credit organizations, or is retained by the retail sector, the proposed system permits the credit grantor to have access to OLRT credit information on the customer at the time of credit extension. Irrespective of who actually grants credit to Mr. Doe (a combination of various credit grantors might all be involved), Doe is free to generate funds transactions throughout the entire OLRT system through the presentation of his universal identifying card for insertion into an on-line terminal device at the point of sale.

OLRT installment credit. Thus far, we have discussed on-line funds transactions mainly for the purchase of consumer goods involving credit lines probably no greater than two or three hundred dollars. But what about using the same basic system to handle a car loan or a mortgage on a house? Ordinarily, this type of loan would be granted from the banking sector or from a savings and loan institution. The loan officer's decision as to whether to grant such a loan, and in what amount, would surely be expedited through OLRT access to the CCF which would provide the officer with valuable information to assist his loan decision and to help him fairly negotiate with the customer. As an added feature (once the loan is granted), the CCF could provide timely reports or warnings to the bank if the customer were to overextend his credit in some other sector of the system. Of course, repayment of the loan could also be preauthorized and take place automatically in predetermined periodic increments as previously discussed.

Operation of the CCF: feedback loops. The computer credit file (CCF) and its function in the system has been briefly discussed, yet little has been said about the operations of the CCF. The authors conceive of the CCF as being an evolutionary outgrowth of today's credit bureau or perhaps an outgrowth of the banks' own customer information files. The proposed CCF is nothing more than a computerized credit bureau, a unit wherein descriptive credit information has been centrally stored in random access

INPUT/OUTPUT FOR THE CCF

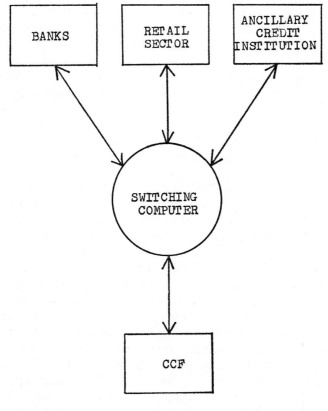

EXHIBIT 7

memory files permitting OLRT inquiry. Exhibit 7 illustrates our concept of the method by which a CCF would obtain and update its customer information.

Since participating banks, retail outlets, and ancillary credit grantors will want to have access to the CCF for reliable, timely information, it will also be in their own best interests regularly to channel pertinent credit information back to the CCF to update and upgrade its information files. The integrated OLRT system would, therefore, include a feedback loop from the CCF users for updating and upgrading the system's information files. Of course, the transmission of updated information to the CCF would not need to be handled in real-time but could be batch-transmitted from the different sectors to the CCF during slack hours.

To summarize this discussion of credit and credit information systems, we draw a distinction between credit information and credit itself. Credit, as a source of funds, may come from an on-line bank, retail outlet, or ancillary credit institution (Exhibit 6). These grantors of credit will be aided in their investigations of customers' credit worthiness through information supplied from an on-line CCF. Credit information which is then generated by these same three sectors, as they develop a history with each customer, is transmitted back to the CCF (Exhibit 7) to update and to upgrade the CCF information.

HOME USERS: BANKING BY PHONE

Just as cash and credit funds transfers can be initiated from terminal locations in retail stores, similar transfers can be initiated from any remote terminal location—whether or not at a point of sale. Touch-tone telephone technology will, in fact, make every telephone unit a potential input device for OLRT funds transfers. All that is needed is for an additional card-reading device to be integrated with the telephone unit; the card reader itself would be essentially the most simple version of the point-of-sale terminal device explained earlier. American Telephone and Telegraph Company's new option, the card dialer, is one simple device, capable of reading hole-punched cards. In this respect, the card dialer is very much like the kind of terminal station that would facilitate banking by phone.

A housewife could initiate funds transfers from her home by simply inserting her identifying card into her telephone card receptacle, keying in the identifying code number of the payee (or inserting another card upon which the payee's identifying number is encoded), and then keying in the transaction amount. The keying-in of data would be accomplished by activating the touch-tone push buttons (which also serve as the dialing instrument for the telephone unit). Once all the data were keyed into the system, the housewife would hear an audio-response, the response being generated by the bank's computer, which would verify orally the numbers she had keyed in. (This audio response mechanism would, of course, be equally adaptable to the point-of-sale terminal devices discussed earlier.) If the audio-response were to indicate a correct input, the housewife would then depress an activator key, which would cause the transaction to be executed. If, on the other hand, the response unit were to indicate an input error to the user, she would simply "hang up" the phone, breaking the connection, and try the whole process over again.

On a monthly basis (just as canceled checks are returned to depositors and document the monthly transactions that went through the bank), the OLRT systems user would receive a computerized statement from the bank listing all transactions generated from the user's identification card, whether the account charges were generated from an actual point of sale, from the user's home, or simply from a roadside pay phone with the card-reading capability. The transactions listing could include the date, time, and amount of each transaction plus information identifying each payee and the point of transaction-entry for each transfer.

The data flow for the bank-by-phone system would take place over ordinary telephone lines. In effect, the insertion of the user's card would simply "dial up" the line to the central switching computer; the switching computer would monitor the transaction from the initial "dial-up."

OTHER ON-LINE PARTICIPANTS

There are obvious advantages for large businesses, service organizations, and other employers to participate in the proposed network (see Exhibit 8). To make payrolls, the company would simply transfer funds from its own account in a bank to the accounts of its employees, using the switching computer to connect all the various banks and accounts involved. Even large payroll transfers could easily be handled by the system, for such mass transactions could be processed at night or during slack periods and in batch form rather than individually and real-time. Essentially, no payroll checks would ever need be prepared, let alone distributed for processing through the banking system. All records concerning payroll computation and funds transfer would naturally be retained by the company, most likely in magnetic tape files. Any need for information pertaining to employee pay or related items, such as withholding tax or social security, could easily be printed on an "as needed" basis.

Other participants in the system would benefit considerably from an automatic and regular input of payrolls into the system. From a cash management standpoint, banks, retail outlets, and other credit-granting facilities should be able to forecast with very good accuracy their own cash flows accruing from clients' preauthorized credit payments. Banks should be particularly happy, for they would be relieved of the burden of payroll-check processing. Private individuals should be pleased because they would be relieved of the bother of check endorsement and deposit or cashing problems. In fact, John Doe would have his money available for spending instantly, with no more worries about whether his mailed deposit reached the bank in time to cover draws against his demand deposit balance.

OLRT funds transfer networks will also be helpful to businesses in processing their payables and receivables. Particular advantage is seen when transfers of very large sums of money are concerned. Interest charges for even one day can be significant with such accounts. Instantaneous funds transfer capability will help corporate cash managers eliminate interest paid on funds "in transfer" and "in clearing."

Government OLRT participation. Obviously, important implications for the Federal Government are suggested by the proposed system. Because of the Government's existing close ties to banks through the Federal Reserve System, it seems likely that the Government will have a type of on-line tie-in to the networks, probably entering the system via Federal Reserve networks, which may be expanded to connect all banks (see Exhibit 8). The Government can be expected to avail itself of the integrated system for management of its tax and loan accounts and for keeping an accurate monitor on the money supply, amounts of credit availability, and similar economic indicators and control mechanisms. Also, as with OLRT business payrolls and funds transfers, the Government can use the system to eliminate its checks and other related paper work.

Perhaps the Internal Revenue Service will connect to the system and monitor employment payrolls, savings account interest, trust fund earnings, and other areas of its interest. There is even the possibility that information in the system's CCF will be traded with comparable information in the files of various Government agencies for the purpose of making all such central files more complete and more accurate.

AUXILIARY SERVICES

An electronic network linking the various economic sectors suggests many related business opportunities which go beyond the mere communication and recording of financial transactions. The authors envision a number of auxiliary business services which could complement the many functional benefits of the OLRT system. The proposed auxiliary-service participants could be service bureau extensions of the on-line banks, credit organizations, retailers, industrialists or, as shown in Exhibit 9, an additional on-line agent specifically established to perform auxiliary services for other on-line participants. The scope of the auxiliary services offered need be limited only by the creative imagination of the service bureau managers. Such auxiliary services might include two general categories: one, the supply of routine accounting information, such as that relating to payrolls, billing, salesmen's commissions, and cost controls; two, the supply of logistical information, such as that relating to inventory control,

ADDITION OF INDUSTRIAL AND GOVERNMENT SECTORS TO SYSTEM

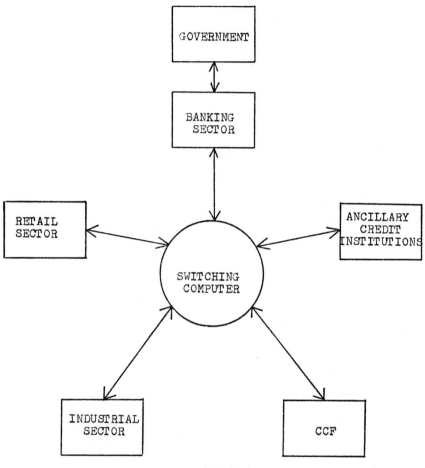

EXHIBIT 8

production control, and market forecasting. Of the two categories, logistical information is naturally the more complicated from a computer hardware and programming standpoint. It is this type of information which will most likely be provided by the auxiliary on-line service bureaus, such as the bureau depicted in Exhibit 9.

Auxiliary bank services. Many of today's banks are already in a position to provide a number of these special services for their clients. For example, previous mention has been given to the concept of preauthorized or auto-

TIE-IN OF THE COMPUTER SERVICE BUREAU

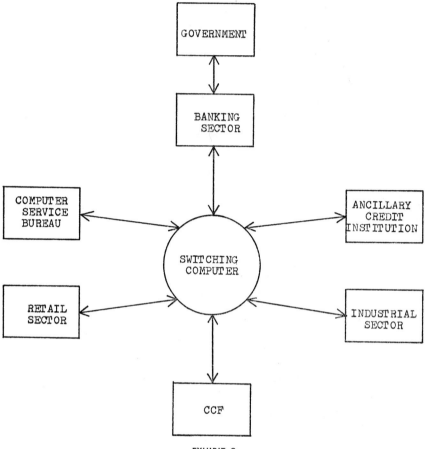

EXHIBIT 9

matic payments whereby, as a customer service, banks might automatically pay customers' bills or installment loans as they fall due without the necessity of the customer actually becoming involved in each transaction.

A payroll service has also been mentioned whereby a large employer could transmit employee payroll information to its bank. As a service, the bank, through its on-line connection with employees' personal accounts, would then transfer funds from the employer's to the various employee accounts. For those companies that do not maintain their own computers, even the calculation and record-keeping phases of payroll processing could be performed by banks as special services. These corporate services need not stop at payroll processing. For example, billing, payments, and all matters of routine financial accounting could be performed for business accounts on a service-fee basis by the on-line banks. (In fact, many commercial banks are offering these types of services today for some corporate accounts. Some banks presently feature special billing and accounting services for doctors and dentists.) Many of the more progressive banks will undoubtedly expand their banking services to include the even more sophisticated services, such as inventory control, traffic management, marketing research, and sales analysis.

Retailers' integrated services. Some of the larger retailers who will possess their own computers will be capable of performing their own EDP and logistic analysis. The on-line flow of OLRT data through the store's own computer system will provide the retailer with the ultimate in management-control-system capability. Exhibit 10 depicts a large retail store, with its own computer system, routing selected OLRT transaction data to its own computer for management control purposes. We see the CTU buffering transmissions to and from the point-of-sale terminal devices. In this case, however, the CTU (or CTU's as in Exhibit 10) is an integral part of the retailer's in-house computer system. The CTU's automatically select which data are to be transmitted to the central switching computer and which data are to be routed to the store's in-house computers for storage and subsequent in-house analysis. Elements of an in-house computer system would include equipment for record keeping and accounting, with perhaps logistics and operations analysis capability as well. For example, when entering transactions into point-of-sale terminal stations, clerks might be required to key in information relating specifically to the merchandise code which would be used only for internal control purposes, analytic purposes, or both, and would not be relayed into the regional system's switching computer (as would the specific funds data pertaining to the transaction). Similarly, clerks could be asked to enter special information, such as the customer's sex and age, for some kinds of merchandise. Subsequent in-house computer analysis of this type of information would be a valuable source of marketing research information. The amount and type of data entered at the point-of-sale terminal are constrained only by the hardware limitations of the terminal device to receive data and the in-house computer system's capability to store and analyze data.

Alternative configurations for stores not large enough to support their own computerized operations could include joint EDP ventures. They would insert their marketing data along with transaction data to the jointly

INTEGRATED SERVICES WITHIN A RETAIL OUTLET

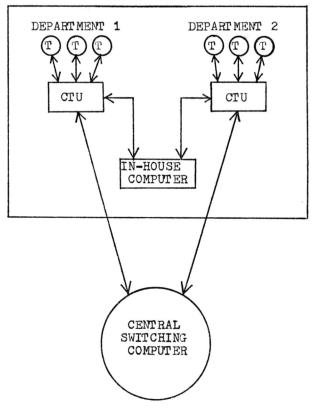

EXHIBIT 10

held central transmission facilities. On a shared-time, fee basis, the joint facility could process the data according to programmed specifications, conceivably performing all the same kinds of EDP analysis for small participating retailers as the in-house computer systems perform for the larger stores.

Independent service bureaus. Should these joint ventures not work out, or should the on-line banks not offer all the computerized services desired by on-line systems participants, or both, the existence of independent on-line computer service bureaus will be inevitable and desirable. In fact, the emergence of on-line service bureaus seems quite likely in order to fill the gap between what the large concerns are able to do for themselves and what the banks and joint-venture concerns are unable or unwilling to do for the smaller participants in the network. These on-line computer service bureaus will be able to perform all the service functions: routine accounting services, logistical information processing, and special marketing research projects.

INTERREGIONAL COMMUNICATIONS

So far in our discussion, we have dealt primarily with data transmission links integrating discrete "market areas." Let us now complete the system by considering a multiregional model. In Exhibit 11, all of the previously introduced system participants are integrated, linked within each discrete area by a regional switching computer. Recognizing that many funds transactions and information transfers will have to cross regional boundaries, we must consider interregional communications.

We can expect the natural growth of several independent communications networks linking across regional boundaries many of the individual sectors. For example, we know that many banks are already interlinked over their own wire networks, either through the Federal Reserve System or through well-established correspondent affiliations. Likewise, national ancillary credit organizations, such as Household Finance Company, have their own on-line network system linking HFC members across the country. Large national retail chains, such as Sears Roebuck & Co. or J. C. Penney, will also find it useful to establish their own national communications networks for reporting and control purposes. These interregional communications networks, linking regional sectors, are depicted by the dotted lines in Exhibit 11.

The authors suggest that many of the interregional communications might, however, take place automatically via the regional switching computers. Such computers would provide a more economical dispatch of interregional data because of the economies of large-scale operations. For example, the credit information bureau in Area 1 might not have sufficient information traffic related to the bureau in Area 2 to justify the leasing of an open line. Sharing of an open line to Area 2 via the switching-computer interregional linkage might prove more economical.

The importance of Exhibit 11, however, is the fact that the OLRT system is not one data network but is really a vast complex of alternative, overlapped, and interrelated networks, such as is the telephone system today. It was with the telephone system analogy to OLRT that we began this discussion. Let us now turn to a slightly more technical examination of the requirements for some of the system's components.

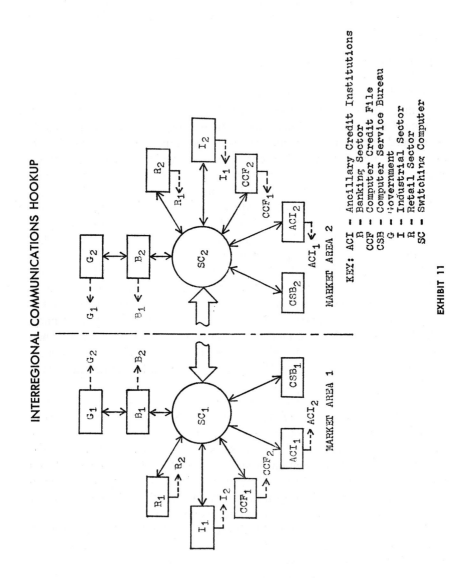

INTERREGIONAL COMMUNICATIONS HOOKUP

KEY: ACI — Ancillary Credit Institutions
B — Banking Sector
CCF — Computer Credit File
CSB — Computer Service Bureau
G — Government
I — Industrial Sector
R — Retail Sector
SC — Switching Computer

MARKET AREA 1

MARKET AREA 2

EXHIBIT 11

CHAPTER III

TECHNICAL CONSIDERATIONS •

THE TECHNICAL ASPECTS of the proposed system can be easily understood by the nontechnical executive. All of the system's components and processes are now in existence, and most of the elements are familiar tools now being used by managers in many industries. While the operation of the various parts of the system may be different from the present uses of these components, the new methods are not difficult to understand, nor are the technological problems involved beyond the "state of the art." As we shall show, the technical aspects of the system are *not* major limiting factors in the development of the system.

The technical problems to be discussed touch upon those areas in which the authors feel critical refinements in present technical capabilities will be important determinants for successful system operation. These problem areas include:

1. The development of a unique numbering system to identify all system users.
2. The perfection of security protection systems and devices to prevent accidental and fraudulent transactions.
3. The perfection of efficient software approaches to file organization for expenditious and inexpensive account access and manipulation.
4. The continuing perfection of OLRT computer hardware itself and the special software programs required to monitor the computers' OLRT operations.
5. The continuing perfection of communications devices and transmit-

ting channels to meet the speed-volume-cost requirements of electronic funds transfer networks.

6. The development of inexpensive, reliable, multifunctional terminal devices to serve the varying needs of potential system users.

UNIQUE NUMBERING SYSTEM

The problem of developing a numbering system to provide a unique number for each potential account holder, both personal and commercial, who will be making transactions within the system is no small one. Techniques used to number and thus to "name" accounts have an important effect upon other technical parts of the system, such as the storage requirements for accounts within computer memories, the time it takes to find an account record in the memory, the type of equipment needed to insure security of account information, the complexity of the computer programming, and, most importantly, the compatibility of different parts of the system. Thus the establishment of a master and universal numbering system must precede many of the other developments required to build the system. Unfortunately, there are major nontechnical problems delaying development and acceptance of such a numbering system. Because there are already a large number of different numbering schemes in existence, there are serious factional disagreements as to which type would be used among various groups (potential on-line participants) who have vested interests in one system or another.

The need for a common system does not become apparent if one looks only at the operations of a single bank, since regardless of what numbering scheme it uses, its customers have similarly numbered account cards, and information reaching the bank from a terminal in any location is prefaced by the customer's number. However, when more than one bank is on-line to the same system, the participating banks have to be operating with the same numbering rules to prevent mistakes, if not chaos. The necessity for a compatible and nonduplicating numbering scheme becomes all the more apparent when several retail stores (with their own account information systems), credit bureaus, and other participants join the system. Finally, once interregional networks are established, it becomes clear that only a well-designed, universally accepted, and nonredundant numbering system will serve the compatibility requirements for network expansion.

So what is needed is a "universal number," one which can be permanently assigned to an individual or company and used by all record-keeping institutions within at least the geographical range of a regional area. (To make a transaction across the country, it would be possible to assign a prefix or suffix to the number to designate the market area of the account holder.) Given the fact that 20 percent of the population moves each year, it may even be impractical to consider a numbering system oriented toward a market area. The best base quantity might be the entire population of the country.

Beyond the obvious requirement of sufficient digits to provide a unique number for every potential account holder (both individuals and commercial entities), several other criteria must be considered in selecting a numbering scheme. Primary among these is the necessity for the number to contain as few digits as possible in order to minimize the significant costs of handling and storage, since literally billions of digits will be involved. Another consideration is the ease of assignment and of reassignment after the death of an individual.

A feature of many computer-based numbering systems which would also be desirable for the "universal number" is the ability to check the validity of the number; that is, whether digits have been transposed in data entry or whether the value of one digit has been altered accidentally in transmission. Such "check" features require additional bits or characters. The checking itself can be done automatically by the computer by means of a checking formula (utilizing "check digits") through which the number is run following transmission.

Numbering schemes. Two basic types of numbering schemes are possible candidates for the universal number: the "numeric" and the "alpha-numeric." Numeric systems involve straight one, two, three sequential numbering and therefore entail the simplest method for unique number assignment. Numbers can be grouped by type if desired. For example, all numbers beginning with the digit "1" could be business accounts. The disadvantage of pure numeric systems is that their use then implies a need for a cross-reference file to determine from the numeric field the name of the account holder. There is also a consequent awkwardness when it is desirable to sort the file alphabetically by names.

The alpha-numeric system, and the "block-alpha-numeric" variant, attempt to accommodate the need for alphabetical organization by relating part of the number to a section of the alphabet. For example, the first two digits of the number might refer to the first letter of the account holder's surname: 01 = *a;* 26 = *z.* The drawback to this type of system is the difficulty of maintaining perfect alphabetical order when new accounts are added to the file (in the case of the plain alpha-numeric) and the need for large gaps between account numbers to allow for file expansion. Some banks, for example, are finding that they need to allow an expansion factor of 64 gaps for each number used.

Filing systems based upon account holders' names, rather than upon numbers, have been developed for some of the recent automated bank files. The Bank of Delaware uses the first five letters of account holders' names, then adds a two-digit number so that duplicate names can be distinguished. This scheme and others which use part of the name and part of an individual's address, zip code, or similar identification are practiced within limited geographical areas but might require an excessive number of extra digits to distinguish all the "Mary Smiths" in the country from one another. Also, each name must be converted into a number to allow records to be sorted or processed by the computer.

Efforts to develop a standardized numbering system. Recognizing this need to develop a universal numbering system, several responsible groups have now begun to study potential solutions. The approach taken by at least one group, the American Standards Association Committee, has been to enlist a membership from representatives of each of the major affected areas of the economy so that the technical or nontechnical concerns of one group are not ignored to satisfy the particular requirements of another. Included on this "X.3 Task Force on Individual and Business Identification" are experts from the field of banking, retailing, and the government, plus others who have a wide background in numbering systems used within many industries.

The social security number. One of the numbering schemes which is receiving the close attention of the several interested groups is the social security numbering system. Obviously, it would be of tremendous advantage to standardize on the basis of a system already in partial use, thereby helping to eliminate some of the costs, regulatory and control problems, and the resistance to change which the installation of a new system would generate. The social security number is particularly advantageous for the following reasons:

1. Almost every adult over the age of 19 has a number (130 million people) now.
2. The Medicare program will result in more social security numbers being issued to older individuals.
3. The adoption of the number for driver's licenses in some states and for high school records in many communities will, if this trend continues, insure that more younger individuals receive numbers.
4. The system is already in place in the filing systems of some institutions. The Mellon Bank in Pittsburgh numbers its savings accounts

with the social security number. Several California banks are examining its use, and the pioneering Bank of Delaware is testing this numbering system in its bank-by-phone operation.

5. One of the prime arguments for the adoption of the social security number is that financial institutions *must* now use the number for reporting income from accounts holders' savings accounts, trusts, and other banking services.

Offsetting these powerful arguments for the use of this system are also a number of deficiencies which the number in its present form cannot meet. For example, the number does not now contain a check digit for insuring errorless transmission. Since a social security number is a "numeric" type of system, there is no built-in reference to the name of the numbered individual. Consequently, a cross-reference index file would be necessary. (However, a cross-reference file will be a necessity in any system to solve problems of lost or forgotten numbers and to allow operators of large files to develop management information systems.) Other technical objections, such as the fact that a file operator in a market area of one million account holders would have to process a nine-digit social security number, when in purely technical terms a seven-digit number would accommodate up to nine million accounts.

Nontechnical objections have also been raised. Some individuals have no number, while others have six or eight. There is the desire of transient workers to avoid reporting income at all. And in the use of multiple numbers, they attempt to avoid reporting too much income ($600 or more) under one number. Another major objection is that although there exists a system for issuing social security numbers, the Government office involved does not proceed at the same pace as does today's economy. Current practice is that the social security office will not even validate a name when one wishes to check a number. A revision of the issuing system, perhaps similar to the Swedish system in which a number is issued to each individual at birth and becomes his social security number and bank account number, would be necessary if the scheme were adopted. Although all business entities today have numbers for various accounting and reporting purposes, it would probably be necessary to renumber these business accounts, using an issued social security-like number for these account holders, with perhaps multiple numbers for decentralized operations or functions.

The initial launching of a full-scale program to number all people and institutions uniformly might incur even more resistance than the recent telephone conversion from letters to numbers or the zip code episode!

However, both of those systems have now been accepted by the public, facilitating customer service and more than repaying individuals for any perceived loss of cherished individuality. Hopefully, the same principle will hold true in the case of a unique numbering system that will facilitate financial transactions. The social security numbering system appears to have the best chance of success.

ACCOUNT SECURITY

Assuming that the social security number is adopted as the universal numbering base, what would prevent a space age version of a check forger from siphoning one's personal account by using a stolen number to make a purchase? Surely none of the security or identification systems in use today are foolproof. (Consider the credit card industry today, for example. New cards must be issued frequently. Disseminating information about lost or stolen cards is slow and clumsy. Thefts and forgeries must be included in the cost of doing business.) A number of tentative answers to this problem have been proposed for the OLRT system of tomorrow. As the operation of necessary technical devices becomes economically feasible, positive identification will soon be possible, removing forever the question of forgeries and criminal impersonators.

Hole-punched card. One relatively simple means of identification is being tested now at the Bank of Delaware. That system involves a card similar to an ordinary credit card, with a few additional features (see Exhibit 12).

The holes scattered through the center of the card are punched representations of the account number, for use in a touch-tone card dialer telephone. Security features of this card include bank-operated coding and punching of cards, nonerasable signature block, and signature-block capability of being signed in fluorescent ink, visible only to a "black light." If one could interpret and duplicate the punched holes, read the signature with one's own black light, and produce a passable forged signature, it would still be possible to use a card which was not one's own, at least during the interval between the loss or theft of the card and the time it was reported missing. (The insertion of a "reported-stolen" card into the system would signal an automatic alarm at the terminal device, deterring even a finder of a lost card from the temptation of trying to use it illegally.)

A number of additional measures could be added to increase the security of this kind of card. Discussed below are a number of proposed security devices and systems, such as embedding a photograph, thumbprint, or both, in the back of the card, requiring that an additional short number or

IDENTIFICATION CARD

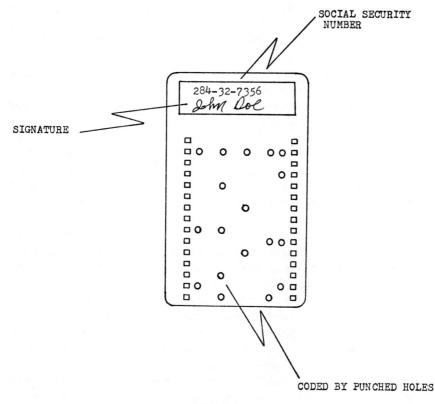

SOCIAL SECURITY
NUMBER

SIGNATURE

CODED BY PUNCHED HOLES

EXHIBIT 12

name be given orally by the card holder, transmitting the account holder's physical description, utilizing facsimile transmission of signatures, and using "voice-print" recognition systems.

Photographs or fingerprints on cards. The use of a photograph or thumb-print further deters but does not completely eliminate the risk of forgery. A forger could manufacture a card with his own photograph or thumb-print in conjunction with another person's hole-punched numbering code.

Extra digits. Another alternative would provide more security but at a greater cost. The requirement is that an additional identifying digit or two be provided orally by the card holder to supplement the digits which are automatically read off his card. The clerk would manually key in these additional identifiers for the customer. These digits would be known only to the customer, and their proper input would be necessary to execute the transaction. The machine-read digits would locate the account and set up the "compare circuits" in the computer to determine whether the correct extra-digit identifier was keyed in to match the digits stored in computer memory. A noncompare condition would indicate forgery, generating an alarm at the point of sale.

Transmission of account holders' physical description. Capable of being used independently or in conjunction with the extra-digit system, the transmission of the account holder's physical description from a stored place in the central information file to the point-of-sale device upon insertion of the card is another security alternative. This description could be received at point-of-sale on a visual display unit (a cathode ray tube), could be received over an audio-response system, or could even be typed out by an on-line electric typewriter. The clerk would then have to check the received description against the customer presenting the card before initiating the transaction.

Facsimile transmission. A more elaborate security measure which could be built into the system is facsimile transmission of cardholders' signatures. Under this plan, a customer would sign his name in the presence of the clerk. The terminal would be capable of scanning the signature and transmitting the signature over a communications system, using the same type of equipment now in use among several banking groups and businesses for transmitting document facsimiles. At the computer end of the system, it would be necessary to compare the signature with a filed signature of the record holder. Present equipment limitations would, however, affect the operational feasibility of this system. The process of scanning a filed signature card and converting it into a code or signal suitable for data transmission is no problem. However, the development of a machine to compare one signature with another will be very difficult, due to the variations in one's handwriting. No commercial hardware is presently capable of selectively determining the *general* form of one's signature while ignoring the *variances* from average that inevitably occur.

An alternative use of "fax-transmission" (facsimile transmission) would be to have the insertion of the account card into the terminal signal the computer to transmit a stored signature back to the terminal so that the clerk could make the comparison of signatures. However, a basic security problem still unresolved by either form of signature facsimile transmission is the potential of forgery. Even assuming that the introduction of electronics and computers to assist in the old problem of signature identification might deter forgers, it does not eliminate them. In addition, the terminal devices capable of transmitting or receiving signatures are costly.

The possibility of facsimile transmission of fingerprints to eliminate forgery problems is being studied. Nevertheless, the problem of comparison of two prints either by a machine or by a clerk still exists, and this solution would require expensive facsimile sending or receiving terminals.

Voice print. Somewhat similar to facsimile transmission, the voice-print concept involves the comparison of the characteristics of one's voice, with stored "records" of one's sound patterns. It has been experimentally shown that words or sounds spoken by an individual can be translated into a pattern which is distinguishable from any other person's pattern. Attempts to disguise a voice, or physiological changes such as colds or sore throats, have no effect upon the basic voice pattern. One's unique voice print can be recognized by electronic equipment regardless of the voice differences apparent to human listeners. The problem of storing one's voice pattern in a form which can be compared with a word or sounds transmitted over a communications system, and the problem of comparing two patterns by means of a machine, prohibit commercial utilization of the idea now. Nevertheless, the technical solution may prove cheaper than comparable measures needed to analyze and compare hand-written signatures, since the voice pattern is more regular.

Assuming that voice patterns can be compared at equal or less cost than fingerprints or signatures, the total equipment requirement would be much cheaper. Voice transmission terminals can be as simple as a telephone. No facsimile reproduction or coding is necessary. A final advantage of the voice-print system would be consumer acceptance, since the only requirement for instantaneous identification would be the statement of a couple of words into an on-line microphone device (a telephone).

FILE ORGANIZATION

Assuming that a system for numbering all accounts and a means of insuring the identity of accounts were developed and economically feasible, how would a store, credit bureau, or bank use the number?

The reason for a number is to provide a convenient means of referencing other on-line information about an account holder. The reason for using a *universal* number is to allow *all* parties within the system to use the most direct and convenient referencing method.

If one examines the types of information that different units within the network must record, it may appear to be inconsistent to attempt to organize them around the basic principle of an account number. The information used by a retail store, such as a customer's age, sex, and purchase history; by a credit bureau, such as employment records, police records, wages, loan history; or by a bank, such as savings account, demand deposit account, loan record, and trust activity, is not similar in content, volume, or frequency of need. How, then, can a uniform system be developed?

Filing concepts. Let us assume that for each individual, information pertaining to one type of his activity—for example, his demand deposit account—is placed in a file folder. This individual's file and all other similar files can then be organized in one of two ways, either by type of information or by the name of the account holder. Retail stores and credit bureaus, with fewer *types* of information to file, have organized their file structure around the principle of a *name*. Banks, however, have made the first subdivision of their file structure that of the *type of information,* such as demand deposits or time deposits. Within that division, they have used the name or number as an organizing basis.

Retail stores and credit bureaus that keep detailed customer records are accustomed to looking at all *types* of information pertaining to an individual name, using this information as the basis for further action. Credit organizations, for example, generally provide all their available data pertaining to an account upon inquiry, and stores often use information about payment history, largest amount outstanding, and number of installment contracts, as the basis for evaluating a customer's ability to purchase an expensive article on an installment plan. Some banks are also realizing the value of organizing information around the principle of the *name* of the account rather than on the basis of the type of information. If it were possible for the banks to retain the ability to locate information by type, when necessary, and yet also have the possibility to convert to a *name* primary file organization, *all* members of the system could share the same filing principle, and could use the account number directly for finding stored information.

Each type of institution could arrange its file folders of information types into a "book," with the name of the book being identical to a customer's name and with an "index" on the first page listing the file folders enclosed. Under this concept, *all* information pertaining to a customer could be subindexed. For example, a bank could locate a customer's name in a book, find through an index the file folder on the customer's banking relationships, go to that file and locate the name of co-signers, go to their books, locate the files for their loans outstanding, and determine the nature and extent of the first customer's liability. It would be possible to keep records on all the legal associates of an account holder, upon past customers, poor customers, employees, potential customers—even records on competing institutions—by using such an indexing system.

The central information file. This use of one basic identifying and cross-referencing scheme (such as a name or number) for locating records and for indexing different types or files of information, is basic to the development of a central information file (CIF). The records within the CIF are of three general types: the cross-reference file, containing the account-holder's name, address, number, and an index to his various types of accounts and financial relationships; the status file, containing all information about the status of a particular type of file, such as a savings account; and a transactions file, which is simply a historical record of all the transactions which have taken place in all the accounts of an account holder, to be used for auditing an account and maintaining a record of activity. Banks would require a fourth file, a control file, to summarize and maintain an up-to-date total for each *type* of information for bank accounting and audit trail purposes.

In describing how files might be organized, we have used terms from manual filing systems, such as libraries. But just as libraries can be automated, this system is adaptable to a computerized network of interconnected files for financial transactions. If properly designed, this automated system will:

- Maintain full control of all information flow within the network.
- Retrieve information from the files within very narrow time limits.
- Accommodate peak demand periods.
- Process, add, or delete information efficiently.
- Maintain full security of access to all information in the system.

The technical design of each CIF within the system must be determined by the number of different files needed, the length of each file in terms of "words" of information, the ability to standardize the information, the frequency of demand for information in each type of file, the frequency of addition or deletions from files, and the time constraints for retrieving a file and processing its information.

Description of a bank's CIF. In order to illustrate a CIF design built upon these considerations and the criteria listed earlier, let us use an example of a bank, the most complex CIF to be encountered in the OLRT system. Let us arbitrarily assign it 100,000 demand deposit accounts, 50,000 savings accounts, 30,000 installment loans, 5,000 corporate trust accounts, and 2,000 personal trust accounts. The bank has developed the concept of a CIF and has organized its records into a cross-reference file for each account holder and into status files for demand deposits, savings, mortgage loans, commercial loans, and for each trust. And the bank has set up a control file for all transactions so that it can maintain its general ledger, cash balance, and so on. Finally, it has determined the desired content of the cross-reference file of each account holder by type of information. Within each separate account file, there would be stored a "field" or "word" of data pertaining to each of the types of information stored on each account. For example, the cross-reference file for each account might begin with a nine-digit field, or word, storing the account holder's social security number. Next would be a field, or word, with the account holder's name. Following these words might be stored other words recording the address, zip code, references to all accounts held by the depositor, references to all banking relationships of the account holder, and so on. Each word within a file would be assigned a fixed number of characters and would require, therefore, a fixed space requirement within the computer's storage bank (nine characters of storage for the social security "word," or 20 characters for the name word, for example).

The space requirement for the total file for each account holder could be an exact figure for each individual account. It could also be an average, or several averages, depending upon whether the account were commercial (with many banking relationships and many types of accounts) or whether it were for a factory employee (with no other files). The choice of "fixed-length files" is determined by a trade-off of the bank's requirements for speed in finding individual account records versus the cost of storage space in its computing facility. If the files are variable in length, the location of one file within a set must be originally determined by finding the beginning of the first file, counting all of its words to find the beginning of the second file, and so on and then indexing the exact location. Although it is possible in this way to make a very compact library, thereby saving storage space, it is also necessary to make a new index each time an entry within one of the files is added or deleted. A fixed-length record, on the other hand, can be located easily (since it is exactly the same size as the other files in the set) by counting in units or blocks. For example, "The file I want is the third one in the set; therefore, it is in the third unit of shelf space."

While the fixed-length file can therefore be more quickly located, a certain percentage of storage space within most files is wasted. In the event a file "runs over," a "note" must be left in the file with an address for the remainder of the records. Even though the inefficient use of space and the steps needed to find an oversize file are objectionable, it appears that most CIF status records and cross-reference records will be stored in fixed-length form, principally because of the necessity for very rapid access to the records.

Reference to individual account files within the CIF will be allowed only to proper authorities. Different levels of security clearance will have to be tailored to the particular CIF in question. For example, the bank teller may be allowed to ask for the demand deposit or savings account file, but only an officer would be allowed access to all the files pertaining to one account holder. Also, outside inquiries such as one from a retail store, asking whether a customer's account balance can accommodate the amount of the purchase, would be answered with *only* a "yes" or "no." The balance itself would not be given. These security measures can at present be built into the system either with software (programming) or with hardware (the design of the terminals and the computer itself). It is expected that most installations in the future will include hardware "barricades" within the file storage area to prevent unauthorized access.

Hardware alternatives for the CIF. To translate these ideas into technical terms, the storage area referred to above is a computer memory. Memories for file storage vary in terms of type and in terms of time required to retrieve a record: As examples, there are a "drums" (the fastest), a "disc file," and a "tape" or "mass memory" (the slowest). The cost becomes less and the capacity, in number of characters of storage, increases in the sequence of examples cited. Considering that the cost of drum storage is generally too high, and the access time of mass memory is too great (the case today), our discussion will focus primarily upon disc files. (It should be noted, however, that memory costs per unit of storage have decreased by a factor of 16 in five years, and that radically new types of internal technology employing cryogenics and laser beams are being seriously researched. Important improvements in the speed and cost of electromechanical devices providing external memory can also be expected.)

The disc file. Having chosen one type of memory, the disc, as the storage unit currently most useful for the CIF configuration, we define it more precisely. The disc, as the name implies, is an object shaped like a long-playing phonograph record, containing tracks (concentric on a magnetic disc) like the record, and capable of holding information in the form of magnetized particles on both its surfaces. The magnetized spots are written or read by a read-write head that is mechanically actuated to locate the correct track on the desired disc.

File organization. The files discussed earlier can be located on the discs either randomly or sequentially. Sequential addressing requires arranging all accounts in numerical order and placing them on the discs in that order. To find an account file, the computer must first look up the disc address of the account in an index. This type of addressing is so machine-oriented —that is, the addressing scheme is designed with more of the characteristics of the computer in mind than those of the users—that it would not provide sufficient flexibility to be of use in a large CIF system. For example, every addition to the CIF would necessitate revision of succeeding portions of the index or establishment of a set of "safety spaces" in the disc with a series of "detour" addresses for all new files entered. In addition, every inquiry for a file requires two steps: first, locating the address in the index, and then going to that address.

The randomly organized disc file eliminates one step in the inquiry process by having the computer "generate" the address directly from the account number. This can be done by a number of esoterically named mathematical techniques. The exact technique to be used depends on the desired degree of "packing" of the storage space (the formula used is checked with an analyzer to insure that efficient use of the disc, up to 85 percent of the disc, is achieved) and the frequency of gaps in the set of account numbers. Even though 99-percent utilization cannot be achieved and though some "chaining" or detour addressing is still required with this technique, it appears that the randomizing method will most satisfactorily meet the demands for speed of access.

The technical discussion has so far concentrated upon the first requirement of the system, a numbering scheme, and upon the last element, the positioning or ordering of the files. In order to complete the discussion, it is necessary to discuss the missing central elements of the computer, the data transmission system, and the terminals.

THE CENTRAL PROCESSING SYSTEM

The function of the computer in the CIF unit is somewhat different from the majority of present computer applications. Today most business data processing tasks are programmed to be processed from start to finish without pause or interruption. The program, or set of instructions, is principally concerned with processing data that are already stored in memory or core, and the processing itself is more critical than the speed or complexities of moving information to and from storage. The system described here, however, is oriented to facilitate the rapid *movement* of information and to service many processing or moving requests. Therefore, the organization of the computer is different from the commonly used computers of today.

The disc-oriented memory already discussed is one example of the differences. A batch-processing job like payroll accounting can use magnetic tape for file storage. The fact that a tape must be searched from its beginning to find a particular piece of information precludes its use in the proposed random access system, since too much time would be lost searching tape.

The OLRT monitor. The most noticeable difference, however, appears in the control programs of the different applications. The OLRT "monitor" must be capable of batch processing during periods of no inquiries in order to fulfill various bank service requirements, such as client payroll service. It must also be capable of monitoring all the input channels to determine when an inquiry has been received, of halting and storing the unfinished batch program, of retrieving, processing, and refiling the requested information in the disc file, and of allocating the available processing time between inquiries if more than one inquiry is received. All of these operations must be performed so quickly that the clerk at the terminal receives information almost as soon as he or she finishes dialing or keying it into the terminal, regardless of how many clerks have made inquiries at the same time. One of the recently developed ways of handling the traffic problem faced by the monitor program has been to divide each inquiry into "segments," and, further, into "pages," which are units of time (microseconds or millionths of a second). The monitor allows one segment into the work area of the computer, and pages within the segment are processed. The monitor then calls for a segment from another inquiry, which is also worked one piece at a time. Many "time outs" occur while the computer works on other inquiries. Although this procedure (known as an "interrupt system") appears to be unduly complex, it allows many inquiries or translations to be worked on simultaneously, while still producing the answer to each inquiry in such short time that to each clerk at the terminals there appears to be *no* delay. In recent years the development of interrupt procedures has been accomplished largely by special programming. However, new random-access computers now have interrupt mechanisms built into the equipment. Any organization using a CIF in the system network will probably require hardware with the described interrupt feature and with an internal processing capacity and "working area" sufficiently large to handle very high volumes of transactions.

Channeling and buffering. The final major difference between a normal batch-processing computer and special OLRT computing equipment is in the treatment of incoming and outgoing information. In most present data processing, input is received in the form of tape and fed into the computer through one "channel." Since the tape unit is mechanically operated (and therefore very much slower in transmitting data than is the computer's ability to process or store the information), many present computer configurations provide a "buffer" or staging area to accumulate information internally from the tape unit and from which the computer can subsequently draw at its own internal rate of speed.

For OLRT applications, a very large number of relatively slow-speed inputs must be received, processed, and retransmitted simultaneously. The buffering operation becomes a very critical function of scheduling and channeling information for internal processing by the central processor. The buffer itself is a sort of first-in, first-out storage shelf where received data are momentarily stored while awaiting the instant when the central processor can handle the information. In OLRT configurations, the expeditious feeding and receiving of information from the buffer area are a considerable problem because of the very large number of input/output channels served by the system.

Devices called multiplexors, which collect the incoming data into a more manageable number of channels (overlapping the communications as with the CTU) have been used in existing OLRT installations. The volume of inquiries into many of the CIF units in the proposed cash and credit system will probably require the use of a *second* computer, a large-capacity multiplexor, whose purpose is strictly to organize and schedule communications into and out of the CIF. This computer would act as a scheduler, editor, switchboard operator, register, and librarian for the incoming and outgoing messages. While this may appear to be complicating the system, separating the communications problem from the processing problem allows development of compact, specially tailored programs and equipment which may be cheaper to install than one all-purpose computer.

The arrangement of all the components leading into the CIF unit may take several forms, depending upon the specific requirements of the OLRT system users. Two of the general plans are shown in Exhibit 13.

An example CIF inquiry. To review the functions of the various hardware components of the system discussed so far, let us process a typical inquiry which has been generated from a remote terminal device and transmitted via the community switching terminal device to the premises of a CIF, a bank, for example. An account number is received by the bank's computer, with an additional notice that the message type is a demand deposit transaction. The computer then generates an address from the account number, goes to the address where the cross-reference file is

TWO ALTERNATE CONFIGURATIONS OF THE CENTRAL INFORMATION FILE

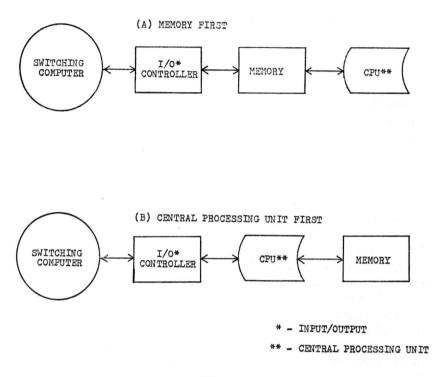

(A) MEMORY FIRST

(B) CENTRAL PROCESSING UNIT FIRST

* – INPUT/OUTPUT

** – CENTRAL PROCESSING UNIT

EXHIBIT 13

kept and searches this file for the index of the demand deposit account. Next, the computer assesses the indicated address, extracts from the demand deposit account file the current status of the account, and moves this information to the computer's working area. The amount in the account is compared with the amount of the purchases which the clerk has dialed into the terminal, and it is found that the funds in the account can cover the amount of the transaction. The account number for the retail terminal (identifying the payee) is retrieved from storage in the same way, and the amount of the purchase is deducted from the customer's account balance and added to the store's. While this operation is being performed, it is simultaneously being recorded on a tape, so that a historical record of all transactions affecting both accounts can be maintained. Thus the bank can control its own account balances, and the transaction can be reconstructed if necessary. An acknowledgment that the transaction has been made is then sent back to the terminal.

COMMUNICATIONS

The communications system chosen for transmitting data from the on-line CIF units to the community central switching computer is a critical element in an electronic transaction system. The considerations in choosing the type of communications system are as follows:

1. The volume of transactions between CIF unit and central switching unit.
2. The format of each transaction input and output.
3. The control procedures used to assure accuracy of each transmission.

Alternative transmission systems. The basic types of communications circuits available include simplex (one-way lines), half duplex (two-way, but only one way at a time), and full duplex (both ways at once). Since a large volume of communications in both directions will be processed between any large CIF and the central switcher, it appears that full-duplex lines will be most adaptable to the system.

Within each category of line circuits, there are also a number of alternative grades, or frequency band widths, which will determine the speed of a transmission. These include telegraph (the slowest), voice, and broad-band grades. Remembering the complexities of multiplexing the input to the CIF computer and of relaying and buffering these data internally for the central processor, it is apparent that transmissions must occur as fast as possible within the limitations of cost. This being the case, the low speed of telegraph circuits (ten characters per second) would create a large queue of partially transmitted messages at the buffer and yet would "starve" the computer. Telegraph circuits, therefore, might not prove to be acceptable communication linkage for high-traffic, real-time requirements.

Voice-grade lines. Voice-grade lines are in widespread use for data transmission at this time, and one of the advantages of their prominence is that a number of different types of terminals have been and can be developed to use the voice-grade lines band width and speed. For example, dataphones, which translate computer information into a form suitable to send over telephone circuits, touch-tone telephones, cathode ray tube visual display units, and some facsimile transmission units, can all use voice-grade lines.

Microwave transmission. By using a broadband communications system, one can transmit a few high-frequency signals like television or divide the bandwidth into a number of narrower voice-grade channels. For example, a microwave system can carry up to 2,700 data messages at a time. One problem that may be encountered with a microwave system is the saturation of available frequencies because of the multiplicity of TV channels, mobile communications systems used by the military, and the like. While CATV lines may free some channels now used by TV (one-half the band width below 1,000 megacycles), the availability of space for microwave systems concentrated in urban areas is limited.

Other possibilities. Several other types of transmission systems present possibilities for the future. The CATV lines would provide a natural network of communication lines to homes when terminals are installed and could be laid to all businesses in the switching area. Another type of "line" which has been proposed is a network of "pipes" which would transmit "millimeter waves" capable of carrying all requirements of homes and businesses; for example, TV, radio, telephone, terminal. Even laser-beam communication represents a possibility within the long-range future.

Of the types of communications which are currently practical, "WATS" lines or dataphone switching service would probably be utilized in the proposed system, the choice being dictated by the volume of transmissions and the cost economics. As Western Union's microwave network is expanded (and if the airlines in the United States decide eventually to install a microwave system for reservations processing), much more reliable knowledge of the costs of large microwave systems will become available. The proposed electronic funds transfer system could feasibly utilize voice-grade telephone lines for the initial installations through a variety of rental or lease plans, converting later to microwave without changing terminals or other communications hardware should a broadband system prove more economical.

The design of the central switching computer itself will be dictated by the volume of transactions which will be processed through it. No single "optimum" design is possible because of the number of businesses which would tie into the switching computer and because the size of each business, in terms of number of transactions each makes, is quite different from area to area and subject to large long-term variations resulting from population shifts and regional economic growth patterns. It is apparent, however, that the switching computer must be oriented almost entirely to very rapid processing time, with a very large work-processing area (core), and need have relatively little storage capability (memory). Its function will be to collect messages from all points in the system and to *route* them to other units in the network, where the changes and manipulation of the data contained in the messages will take place.

TERMINAL DEVICES

The final hardware requirement of the system, the terminals and other equipment located at the retail stores, industrial plants, and various other places, may in fact be the most complex requirement.

Touch-tone terminals. Relatively simple touch-tone telephone units, equipped with card-dialer attachments to receive insertion of identification cards, are now operational and, in the initial stages, should provide adequate terminal facilities for organizations such as small retail stores.

One very serious drawback to present touch-tone installations is the problem of error control. In a normal telephone, dialing a number causes a series of pulses much like Morse code (except that each pulse is of equal length) to be sent over the line after being "modulated" up to a transmittable frequency. Touch-tone accomplishes the same end by transmitting different frequencies for each number rather than different patterns of pulses on the same frequency. In either system, unless there is a very large investment in special electronic equipment, errors can easily occur in both the transmission and the receiving of signals. This is an intolerable situation, since people's account balances and other financial records are jeopardized.

Other devices. One approach which can be taken is to design special types of terminals that can accomplish more and different jobs than can the simple card-dialer telephone. Passbook-savings-posting machines, an example of this type of terminal, as well as many of the new kinds of terminals now in use for other purposes could be adapted for a wide variety of uses within the system. For example, the cathode ray tube unit, a special TV-like device, could provide a visual display of the information requested from information files. This display device would be activated by making an information inquiry on an attached input unit, such as an on-line typewriter keyboard. With this device on-line to the system we propose, bank officers and retail and credit-company managers could be provided a visual means of receiving instantaneously all the necessary information contained in the system's CIF files pertaining to a customer. Other units could be designed to combine the function of the present cash register with an electronic system for inventory control as well as to provide a terminal for the CIF unit. All of the terminals described previously have one disadvantage—high cost. A teller terminal, for example, rents today for about \$350-\$435 monthly, compared with \$5.50 for a touch-tone telephone.

The problems of terminal design, which include the development of cheaper multipurpose devices and the improvement of touch-tone error control, will undoubtedly be solved in the near future through the concentrated efforts of many manufacturers to upgrade their products to meet the needs of real-time computer systems of all types. In the interim, present touch-tone telephones in the area equipped to use them will work quite satisfactorily if the computer is programmed to give a vocal or visual confirmation of all information which it receives from the terminal as a check measure.

As has been shown throughout this chapter, technological difficulties are not a major deterent to the rapid installation of electronic cash and credit systems. In the following chapters, we will examine in some detail the operations of future OLRT participants in an effort to understand other relevant considerations that will affect OLRT acceptance and installations.

CHAPTER IV

THE BANKING SECTOR •

O PPORTUNITIES for the banking community to capitalize on the proposed electronic cash and credit system through the development of metropolitan and regional arrangements are limited only by the imagination of bankers themselves. As an article on the checkless society notes, " . . . the technology and the economic justification to develop these systems are here now."[1]

Already bankers have shown evidence of creatively applying OLRT capability to their activities. Several savings banks, such as the Howard Savings Institution in Newark, New Jersey, have proved the feasibility of real-time operations. A number of commercial banks, such as First National City Bank of New York, have provided leadership in new approaches to consumer credit. Bank-owned or -sponsored credit cards, such as Bank Americard, have pioneered in enabling the consumer to enjoy the advantages of consolidated billing through the most logical financial institution. The particularly significant steps taken toward a total financial-services package, as envisioned by the Bank of Delaware, have expanded the vision of bankers in this country and abroad.

Equipment developments and banking trends that are providing bankers with opportunities to apply OLRT capabilities include the following:

[1] Robert Head, "The Checkless Society," *Datamation,* March 1966.

1. The equipment is available now for operation of the system. Many operations have been proved economically feasible at today's costs. Of greater import for the future is that technological breakthroughs and production efficiencies by computer manufacturers are making on-line, real-time computer systems the desirable purchase for tomorrow's banking.

2. Check volume at its present rate of growth, according to the American Bankers Association, will rise in the next five years from 17 billion checks to over 22 billion checks. While faster processing of checks by newer computers represents one answer, the desirable economic alternative lies with the system we propose, which will eliminate the vast majority of checks.

3. Banks have moved into consumer credit at an increasing rate since the early 1950's. Direct consumer financing, with its higher interest rates, has provided banks an opportunity to realize higher yields on loans while satisfying a public need. The electronic cash and credit system offers an opportunity for banks to expand this profitable application of their asset investment.

4. The proposed electronic cash and credit system will allow banks to offer more sophisticated and extensive automated customer services, both in the fields of statistical analysis and of financial payments.

5. In an industry where corporate image and customer convenience have been differentiating factors to secure and retain accounts for basically uniform financial services, banks of any size participating in an electronic cash and credit system have a unique opportunity to gain or enhance a leadership position by providing a full-service, low-cost package so needed by today's consumer.

GROWTH OF THE CHECK AS A PAYMENT MEDIUM

The check-processing department has emerged in the past 20 years as the largest department in the average bank in terms of personnel and equipment investment costs. Encoders, proof machines, sorters, and computer systems, together with expensive staffs to man them, comprise the major investment in dollars and talent by the banking industry to stay abreast of the flood of checks today. There are only a few banks in the country today where the "factory" operation of check processing is not a significant concern for bank management. There are fewer still where senior operating executives are not anticipating with dread the threatened flood of paper documents yet to come. In the next five years, the American

Bankers Association estimates check volume will expand another 33 percent, to 22.7 billion checks. The electronic cash and credit system offers a positive alternative to this problem by eliminating the majority of checks. A brief review of demand deposit accounts will help to define the magnitude of the problem and to support the conclusion that the real solution lies in completely eliminating checks as a payment medium.

With the increasing affluence of our society, our economy has trended away from currency toward the more convenient payment mediums of the check and the charge card. Exhibit 14 points up the growth in the number of demand deposit accounts.

A natural growth in the number of accounts has resulted from higher incomes and an increasing population. In addition, banks have spurred the growth of checks by using special accounts as a marketing tool to gain and retain customers. The emphasis on promoting individual checking accounts as a source of funds has been particularly strong since the early 1950's. Sharp-penciled corporate treasurers and controllers have reduced their unproductive demand deposit balances and shifted these funds to more profitable short-term uses. But while the banks were able to offset the loss in funds of corporate accounts by the increase in individual accounts, this has necessarily been accompanied by a huge increase in the volume of checks processed:

Year	No. of Checks (Billions)
1945	5.3
1950	7.0
1955	9.5
1960	12.7
1961	13.5
1962	14.3
1963	15.1
1964	16.0
1965	17.0
1966 (est.)	18.0
1970 (est.)	22.7

Source: American Bankers Association.

GROWTH IN NUMBER OF DEMAND
DEPOSIT ACCOUNTS

Year	Population	Number of Demand Deposit Accounts*	Number of Accounts per 100 Population
1936		22,109,000	17
1945	140,468,000	35,622,000	26
1955	165,931,000	52,212,000	31
1964	192,119,000	70,895,000	37

* Includes individuals, partnerships, and corporations.
Source: Federal Deposit Insurance Corporation *Annual Report.*

EXHIBIT 14

In order to examine the relative growth in checking accounts and check activity, the 1945 population and check statistics have been used as a base for comparison with 1964 (see Exhibit 15).

Costs of check processing. The large volume of check processing is accomplished at a considerable cost to most banks. In 1964, the New York Federal Reserve Bank prepared a functional cost analysis based on data gathered from 279 participating member banks in the First, Second, and Third Reserve Districts. The performance characteristics of the high-earning banks, or upper quartile, are particularly relevant for examination, because they indicate that for banks in the $50-million to $650-million deposit groupings, the demand deposit expense varies from 24 percent to 45 percent of total portfolio and deposit expenses. (Part of the variation is due to the relative amounts of time deposits to total deposits, part to statistical reporting.) It is quite clear that demand deposit expenses offer a major opportunity for cost reduction.

Several of the medium- and large-size banks cooperating in our research effort indicate per-item check processing costs between eight and ten cents on checks drawn on them. These bank figures are from banks which are completely computerized in the usual definition of the term.

Accounting centers. It is useful in our examination of the expanding check volume to point out that the number of banks (the bank is the basic

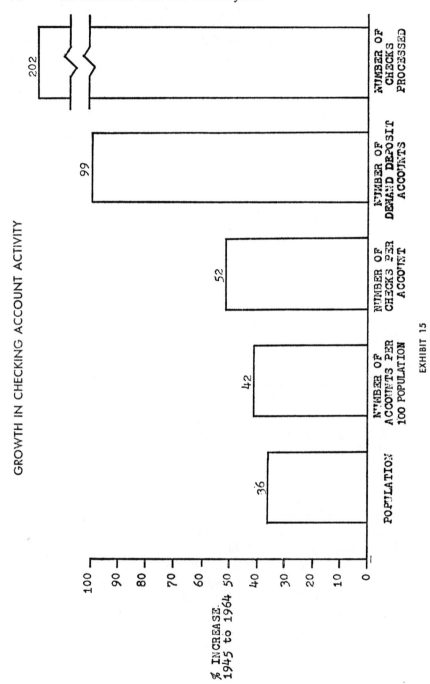

GROWTH IN CHECKING ACCOUNT ACTIVITY

EXHIBIT 15

statistical unit for check processing) has not changed materially since 1945:

Year	Number of Banking Offices	Number of Branches	Number of Banks
1945	18,881	4,168	14,713
1950	19,851	5,158	14,693
1955	21,676	7,391	14,288
1960	25,105	11,106	13,999
1961	26,002	12,043	13,959
1962	27,029	13,078	13,951
1963	28,369	14,277	14,092
1964	29,726	15,445	14,281

Source: Federal Deposit Insurance Corporation *Annual Report*.

The majority of banks with branches have consolidated their check-processing operations at the home office. Since the absolute number of banks has not increased, the load on the *average* bank has tripled since 1945. Several large banks in the nation are each processing over 300 million checks per year. Likewise, the pressure to plan adequately for the processing of checks is equally great for small banks seeking to maintain and expand their operations.

While these statistics are familiar to most of the banking community, they serve to substantiate the conclusion that checks as a payment medium are becoming an increasing problem to banks. In light of technological advances, cost developments, and convenience trends, checks as a payment medium appear outdated. This situation will become increasingly burdensome unless certain alternative programs are implemented.

Faster processing of checks. As the volume of checks to be processed has grown, banks have taken several measures to expedite processing. Banks identified accounts with numbering codes as the paperwork load made processing on a personal basis impossible. Unfortunately, these codes are in many cases unique to a bank or to a region, and it is only recently that banks have cooperated in a study for a unique, universally accepted number for each account.

In the 1950's, the development of Magnetic-Ink-Character-Recognition (MICR) encoding enabled banks to expedite check processing in conjunction with first- and second-generation computers. By the early 1960's, MICR had been adopted widely enough that over 85 percent of all checks processed could be processed by high-speed computers. At the present time, computer systems manufacturers are assisting banks with the check-processing volume by the introduction of greater-capability third generation computers and by systems analysis specialists. OLRT technology now provides equipment capability for electronic transfer of funds.

Initial steps to reduce burden: no check return. W. P. Livingston, vice president of Bankers Trust Company, New York City, in a paper at the 1965 American Bankers Association Automation Conference, proposed that banks stop moving checks. He suggests that the paying banks retain the checks as was formerly the case. Under his proposal, a customer would only receive a statement listing sorted checks by serial number, date paid, and amount. The banks would store the checks and retrieve them on customer request. In a pilot study conducted by Bankers Trust over a 30-month period, only some 25 checks per 10,000 had to be retrieved for customer reconciliation purposes. This is a very favorable indication of the desirability of his proposal and of the credibility of the contention that customers really don't need, nor apparently desire, to possess canceled checks as proof of transaction.

Consolidated billing. The payment of only one check per month to American Express, Carte Blanche, or Diners' Club in payment for multiple purchases of goods or services is a familiar example of consolidated billing. Banks have also entered this field of operations. They have found the dual advantage of reducing check volume and of increasing earnings potential through agreements with retail establishments. Bank Americard is now honored in over 50,000 locations. Valley National Bank, Phoenix, Arizona, has recently issued 224,000 charge cards, which may be used by consumers in over 4,500 establishments covering 71 types of businesses in 105 communities. Under these charge account plans, the customer writes only one check to cover all his month's charges, greatly reducing the number of checks passing through the banking system.

Preauthorized payment. Many employers have entered into agreements with their employees to credit automatically the net payroll amount to the employee's personal bank account without a payroll check being issued, deposited, or processed. A number of insurance companies have plans whereby the policyholder's bank account is automatically debited and the company account credited for insurance premiums on specified dates.

There are several more examples of the concept of preauthorized payments, such as automatic savings plans and utility billing, but the examples cited should be sufficient to prove that preauthorized payment plans are a helpful device in reducing check flows and represent an important step in psychologically preparing people and institutions for the checkless society envisioned by the authors.

Promise for the future. Thus developments by the banking community have attempted to reduce the volume of check activity. But now complete elimination of the majority of checks processed may be accomplished through the implementation of the proposed electronic cash and credit system. Electronically transmitted data that indicate debits and credits to demand deposit accounts directly from payment terminals in retail establishments or homes via OLRT computer technology is possible. Assuming a bank develops adequate audit trails, safeguards against loss of data, sufficient customer identification security measures, and appropriate statements and proof of charges (all of which are in the realm of present capability), any bank with the proper computers could eliminate the burden of check processing as it presently exists.

Advantages of an OLRT system for banks are as follows:

1. The system would draw the depositor into a closer relationship with his bank by providing a more convenient consolidated payment system for the depositor.

2. Major savings will result eventually from reduced personnel costs. While the system will require substantial expenditures for development of the internal banking systems, the computer investments and data transmission costs can be viewed simply as expenditures made in lieu of additional or faster check-processing equipment. For example, one medium-size Eastern bank reduced its check-processing staff by one-third (including additions of computer personnel) when it switched from posting machines to computers. It was also able to reduce the proof and transit staff by a net of 60 percent after consolidation of the branches and computerization of its operations.

3. Operations will necessarily be more dependent on machines rather than on large staffs. This may be beneficial in the event of a major work stoppage. For example, we cite the January 1966 transit strike in New York City. During the strike, there was no appreciable drop in the volume of check activity. However, during this same period, in spite of Herculean efforts by the staff members who did reach their banks (at a substantial cost in overtime), the production of most check-processing departments dropped disastrously.

OLRT transfer of funds and credit offers significant promise for future efficient banking operations.

BANK POSITION IN CONSUMER CREDIT

Banks have been expanding their activities in the consumer credit area at a rate faster than the expansion of overall consumer credit. Pressures for investments of funds derived from excess internally generated funds of corporations have contributed to this trend. In addition, consumers' needs for funds provide an attractive market for investment yield.

In the 1960-65 period, commercial banks in New York City averaged slightly under 5 percent on commercial loans, but it has been possible to achieve effective interest rates of 9 percent on personal installment loans. With the costs of obtaining funds rising, as evidenced by the rates of interest for certificates of deposit and time deposits, the expansion of consumer loans has been an avenue for improved profitability for the banks. It is likely to remain so.

Exhibit 16 illustrates the relative historical expansion of total consumer credit and the major segments thereof. During the period between 1950 and 1964, the total of consumer credit in current dollars (unadjusted) expanded over 250 percent while the population was increasing only 26 percent.

The expansion of commercial bank activity into consumer credit is illustrated by Exhibit 17.

Banks have made it considerably easier to obtain personal loans. For example, First National City Bank of New York (FNCB) offers "Ready Credit." Under this loan arrangement for convenience, a borrower establishes a line of credit with FNCB and then uses special checks anywhere to create and add to the amount of his loan. First National Bank of Arizona, according to an article in *American Banker,* is offering a service called "Credit Reserve Checking Account," which is quite similar in many respects to FNCB's "Ready Credit." The Arizona bank pioneered in the use of the zip application form, which categorizes the various types of necessary data and requires the customer only to fill in "code numbers," thereby accelerating the processing and scoring of the credit application.

Banks are promoting direct consumer loans because the yields are better than financing the intermediary merchandisers. In order to attract the average consumer, they are making it easier for him to borrow. An electronic cash and credit system employing the speed, convenience, and accuracy of OLRT technology permits both goals to be accomplished.

Credit records. A relevant aspect of the increasing position of banks in consumer credit is that banks are maintaining substantial credit files on individuals. Banks are capable of providing excellent credit data on the

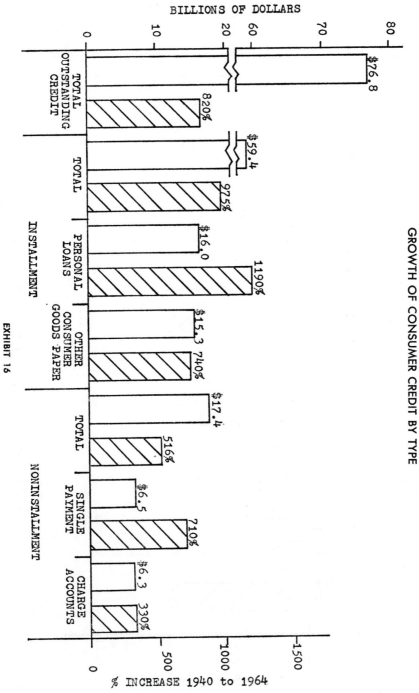

BILLIONS OF DOLLARS

GROWTH OF CONSUMER CREDIT BY TYPE

TOTAL OUTSTANDING CREDIT — $76.8 — 820%

TOTAL — $59.4 — 975%

INSTALLMENT

PERSONAL LOANS — $16.0 — 1190%

OTHER CONSUMER GOODS PAPER — $15.3 — 740%

TOTAL — $17.4 — 516%

NONINSTALLMENT

SINGLE PAYMENT — $6.5 — 710%

CHARGE ACCOUNTS — $6.3 — 330%

% INCREASE 1940 to 1964

EXHIBIT 16

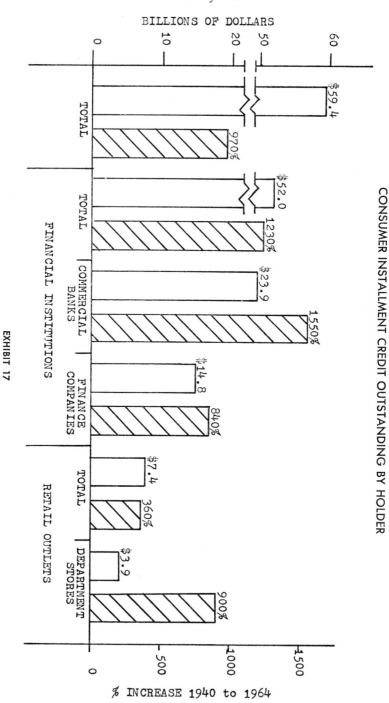

CONSUMER INSTALLMENT CREDIT OUTSTANDING BY HOLDER

EXHIBIT 17

customers they serve because of information obtained in granting a borrower a loan or line of credit. In addition, banks have access to other financial data on a current basis, such as account balance in the case of a customer with a demand deposit account. To a certain extent, credit bureaus and the banks are duplicating the creation and maintenance of credit files. Further, both institutions are presently purchasing computers to achieve faster access to, and updating of, these credit records. There is some exchanging of data between the two institutions. However, it appears clear that as banks add to their credit records, a more permanent relationship could be profitably established with the credit bureaus.

The electronic cash and credit system offers a bank the potential opportunity of exchanging complementary data with credit bureaus on an on-line basis. Thus the unique proprietory interests of each party would be served. Banks may also offer credit information as a revenue service to retail merchants. The banks could also be providing themselves with credit verification in cases where they extend the credit.

CHARGE ACCOUNT BANKING

From 1950 to 1965, over 100 banks successfully ventured into charge account banking. Each month, an increasing number of communities are being serviced by leaders in commercial banking who are introducing bank credit card plans. The concept is the same as that of the major credit cards. However, a major difference is that bank credit cards are aimed for use in a wide variety of retail establishments to cover the whole spectrum of consumer purchases. They are also effective only within the bank's geographic area of commerce. An electronic cash and credit system, with the banks issuing the unique identification cards, would enable every participating bank to be a charge account bank through real-time operation.

Advantages of bank credit card plans. One advantage of bank credit card plans is that check volume is reduced because of the consolidation of billing. Bank credit cards permit a customer to make multiple purchases in retail establishments, purchases which he pays for with one monthly check to the bank.

A second advantage is that the charge cards represent a substantial profit-generating activity for a bank. This assumes that the bank is reasonably prudent in issuing the cards and efficient in processing transactions. Banks discount from 3 to 7 percent of credit sales by merchants in return for handling the billing and credit operations and for the immediate crediting to the retailers' accounts of the net amount. In addition, bank interest charges to the credit card holder for the unpaid balance of customer charges outstanding at month-end vary from 0.5 to 1.5 percent per month, averaging over 1 percent. Overall net yield, according to a survey of member banks in the Charge Account Bankers Association, ranged from 3.5 to 12 percent, averaging 7 percent.

A third benefit of such credit card plans is the attendant increase in demand deposit accounts maintained with the sponsoring bank by the retail merchants participating in the bank credit card plan. Also, a bank card plan in a community usually attracts additional individuals as depositors and enlarges the previous relationship of depositors with their bank.

Still another benefit relates to the credit history which the sponsoring banks can develop concerning card holders. Together with other information which they normally can acquire (demand deposit balance, gross earnings, mortgage balance, and so on), credit cards permit a bank to complete a valid credit profile on each of its customers.

Finally, one of the most important advantages is the additional prestige that the bank gains. Today, the emphasis of most banks is to provide full-service banking; that is, all the financial services a customer would want. A credit card to simplify consumer purchases and payments, widely accepted and desired by merchants and handsomely profitable in its own right, is a strong marketing tool to retain present bank customers and attract new ones. The increasing number of banks that are issuing charge cards testify to the success of this service and its enthusiastic public reception. Based on a survey of the membership of the Charge Account Bankers Association conducted in the spring of 1965, there were at that time approximately 70 bank charge plans with more than four million individual card holders who were expected to charge over $450 million in 90,000 retail outlets during 1965. In just the first three months of 1966, according to articles appearing in the *American Banker,* new bank charge plans will have added over 1.4 million card holders who can purchase in 21,000 retail establishments by year-end. Banks such as American Fletcher National Bank and Trust Company (Indiana), First Wisconsin National Bank, Seattle First National Bank, and Valley National Bank (Arizona) have announced plans to issue over 200,000 cards each.

Some bankers claim that bank charge plans are just for the big banks "that can afford that sort of thing." Referring again to reports of the Charge Account Bankers Association, it appears that large numbers of issued cards and high volume of transactions are not the essential criteria for success. "Banks with volume as low as $500,000 per year and as few as 200 participating merchants and 5,000 cardholders report good operating profits."[2] Essentially, most of the banks in the country that are in retail banking could qualify.

Electronic transfer a logical next step. The offering of bank credit cards is an increasingly important and desirable bank service to complement purchasing habits of consumers. Bank charge plans permit smaller merchants to offer credit at a reasonable cost where they were otherwise unable to support credit service themselves. Added convenience is provided consumers by permitting them to shop in many stores while only using one card. Customers can repay charges on an installment-loan basis if they desire. In addition, many plans permit card holders to obtain cash advances upon presentation of their cards at a branch bank.

Operation of, and planning for, such a large number of bank credit card plans is essentially the initial step in organizing an electronic cash and credit system. Processing of transactions in an OLRT system is quite similar to most of the bank charge card plans, as far as the consumer is concerned. Additional advantages of an OLRT system are expanded customer and merchant service capability and the total elimination of check processing. From the Bank of Delaware to the Bank of Hawaii, from the Bank of Louisiana to the Michigan National Bank, bankers are taking the first steps toward the electronic cash and credit system. The profitability of these plans and their widespread public acceptance demonstrate the feasibility and desirability of OLRT transfers as the banking system of tomorrow.

STATE OF AUTOMATION IN BANKING

Computer automation was introduced into banking operations to meet the growing demands of check processing. Now that this application has been generally adopted and the impact of the computer appreciated, several other areas of banking have benefited from computerization. Savings accounts, mortgage loans, consumer loans, commercial loans, personal trust accounts, and many of the internal operations of the banks, such as payroll and personnel records, are typical of the higher-priority areas that have been computerized. Having automated their basic services, many banks progressed to offering a whole range of customer services, both analysis and accounting. The use of these services, as a marketing tool for banks, has increased substantially in the last few years because of the advantage of increasingly lower costs of providing these services by banks with computers or computer time available.

[2] E. J. Brennan, Jr., "Another Look at Charge Account Banking," *The Credit World,* November 1965.

BANKS WITH COMPUTERS, IN PROCESS OF INSTALLATION, OR ON ORDER—
APPLICATIONS CONVERTED, BEING CONVERTED, OR PLANNED

	All Banks Reporting	Size of Bank (millions of dollars)			
		$10-$50	$50-$100	$100-$500	Over $500
	Percent	Percent	Percent	Percent	Percent
Special checking	97	100	98	99	94
Regular checking	99	100	96	100	100
Savings accounts	78	89	71	78	75
Proof & transit	63	76	56	57	77
Consumer loan	84	87	79	85	84
Mortgage loan	60	52	53	60	68
Commercial loan	32	22	20	32	48
Personal trust	58	25	46	65	83
Corporate trust	54	21	39	61	74

EXHIBIT 18

The growing volume of checks and the successful application of computer capabilities to other banking operations and services have created a dynamic effect in the banking industry. The "have nots" are rapidly becoming "haves" either through the purchase of computers or through the use of computers of correspondent banks, bank cooperatives, service bureaus, or joint ventures.

An indication of how far computer automation has progressed is noted in a nationwide survey of automation in banking conducted by the American Bankers Association (ABA) and published during 1964. Several of the tabulations abstracted from this survey are of particular significance to our study (Exhibit 18). These figures indicate that despite differences in size, banks have almost, or are in the process of, completely computerizing their check-processing operations. In the four areas of mortgage loan, commercial loan, personal trust, and corporate trust, it appears that the larger banks are progressing much faster. In view of the relative position that the large banks hold in terms of dollar volume of operations, it is pertinent to examine what their future plans were in 1964 (Exhibit 19).

PERCENTAGE OF REPORTING BANKS RESPONDING POSITIVELY

	Size of Bank (millions of dollars)	
	$100-$500	$500 and Over
	Percent	Percent
Replace computers with newer ones	48	53
Add more computers	58	80
Investigate real-time, on-line systems*	49	61
Install more random-access memory*	41	45
Use data transmission equipment*	37	56

* Note that there is a general trend in these plans toward acquiring the capability for OLRT operations necessary for an electronic cash and credit system.

EXHIBIT 19

An approximate indication of the trend in computer usage derived by A.B.A. from its survey is given in Exhibit 20.

The trends reported in the A.B.A. survey have followed predictions as indicated by data published by NABAC (The Association for Bank Audit, Control and Operation) in its *1965-1966 Directory of Bank Automation* and based on a survey completed in late October 1965 (see Exhibit 21).

The results of surveys conducted by the two foremost representative bodies of the banking industry lead us to conclude that by 1970 the banks that conduct over 90 percent of the dollar volume of banking operations in this country will own computers or have arrangements for computer operations off premises. Computer capability is a basic requirement for implementing an electronic cash and credit system in any metropolitan or regional area, and it is clear that this capability will be available.

Random-access central information files and OLRT data communications capability are two essential computer characteristics for the system we propose. The NABAC *Directory of Bank Automation* lists 343 bank computer installations by application and computer characteristic, including 31 of *Fortune's* top 50 banks. Ninety-eight of these have random-access capability. Of this total, 57 installations are in banks which have computerized both checking accounts and savings accounts; 34 are in banks in which only checking accounts are computerized. Twenty-nine banks have on-line data communications capability, including 23 which also have random access.

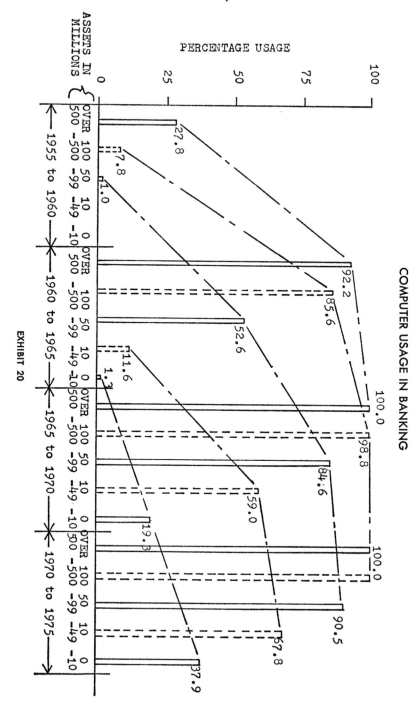

EXHIBIT 20

BANKS USING COMPUTERS (BY RESOURCE CLASS)

Resource Class (millions of dollars)	No. of Banks in U.S.A.	No. of Banks Reporting	No. of Banks with On-Premises Computers	No. of Banks Using Off-Premises Computers	Total Banks Reporting Use of a Computer No.	Percentage
$100 and over	368	248	237	2	239	97
$50-$100	313	119	60	18	78	65
$25-$50	617	192	37	50	87	45
$10-$25	2,125	244	4	58	62	25
Under $10	10,253	267	—	56	56	21
	13,676	1,070	338	184	522	

Source: 1965-1966 Directory of Bank Automation

EXHIBIT 21

Some bankers may express skepticism of the equipment feasibility of this concept. However, progressive spokesmen in the banking industry have pointed to the potential for on-line, real-time banking. Banks such as the Bank of Delaware are demonstrating the feasibility and desirability of on-line, real-time banking for commercial banks based on central information files. Industry leadership in the future, with the attendant benefits of attracting depositors and additional revenue operations, will be attained by the banks who implement OLRT banking for all the financial, credit, and information needs of their market areas.

BANKING SERVICES FOR CUSTOMERS

Banks acquired computers to reduce the burden check processing placed on bank capacity. Aggressive bankers are offering this computer capability as a service to customers for handling accounting chores and analysis problems. The automated customer services being offered have the double advantage of differentiating a bank by means of the additional services provided and of giving the bank an additional source of fee income at little incremental cost. Since a substantial volume of transactions for retail businesses would flow through the bank's computer on a real-time basis under the system we propose, banks will be given a unique opportunity to expand the number and variety of profit-producing services offered to the commercial community.

Most banks offering automated customer services have started with payroll and account reconciliation. So called lock-box service, providing for processing of payments to the merchant's account and preparation of accounts-receivable status reports, is another common program. One major bank now has over 400 customers for this service.

The results of a survey published in the *American Banker* indicate that imaginative bankers, either independently or in cooperation with computer manufacturers, are beginning to provide a wide spectrum of accounting and analysis services. The Harvard Trust Company in Cambridge, Massachusetts, prepares a daily revenue analysis for a local hospital. Valley National Bank in Phoenix, Arizona, is offering "Autodata," an automated inventory control system specifically for automobile dealers. First National City Bank of New York has a real estate information/collection service, which eliminates the bulk of accounting operations for tenant billing and collection, as well as produces several analytical reports for management control. The Bank of Delaware is marketing a complete accounting service for physicians and other professional individuals. The Philadelphia National Bank is using its computer for student scheduling and school district account processing. Several banks have analysis applications available for customers, such as the cost, product, customer, and job analysis services of the American National Bank and Trust Company of St. Paul, Minnesota.

These examples are just a few of the wide variety of possible creative uses of computers. Some common factors about automated customer services stand out:

1. Banks of any size can offer special computer services provided they have computer time available. The Bank Computer Center of Connecticut, Inc., a data processing center jointly owned by nine small banks, offers several services. At the other extreme of bank size is Bank of America with its Direct Billing Service for transfer of funds on a preauthorized-payment basis.

2. Customer services being marketed have a low incremental cost because the economic justification for the computer equipment largely rests on demand deposit applications.

3. Substantial demand for these services by firms of all sizes is generated because of operating savings resulting from bank processing and the opportunity to use computer analysis capability. United California Bank has over 500 customers for its EDP services.

4. Automated customer services have a significant potential for producing income for banks. Revenue is generated by discounting direct billing from the use of demand deposit balances maintained, from fees for particular services, or from combinations of the above. National Shawmut Bank of Boston says, " . . . acceptance by corporate customers of new EDP services gives promise of a meaningful increase in fee income in the years ahead." The Pittsburgh National Bank estimates that by 1968 half of its computer time will be devoted to customer service assignments processed on a fee basis.

5. The expansion of automated customer services for the commercial entity, coupled with consolidated billing under various charge plans and preauthorized payments for the consumer depositor, substantiates the trend toward the provision by banks of the integrated financial services package we envision.

Thus we see an ever-increasing number of banks capitalizing on their unique position in the monetary exchange process and on their computer capability to attract commercial, professional, and consumer depositors and to produce a profit by offering automated customer services. Since the electronic cash and credit system increases the flow of transactions through a bank on a real-time basis, it also increases the capability of banks to provide accounting and data analysis services to depositors. In turn, it offers an attractive source of revenue for increased profits.

A PILOT OLRT OPERATION: THE BANK OF DELAWARE

The experiment conducted at the Bank of Delaware, in Wilmington, represents the closest approach yet devised, at the time of this writing, to an operational electronic cash and credit system.

In a joint venture with IBM and AT&T, the bank has developed the equipment and the systems work needed to provide on-line, real-time banking services for a select group of customers and is planning to expand its system in the near future to accommodate an increased range of services and many more participants—both retail firms and account-holding customers.

In its present stage of development (1966), a group of 200 customers, having special identification cards, can use their cards to make purchases in a local retail store chain, Storm Shoes. This initial test provides for an audio-response acceptance, refusal, or request for re-entry of a purchase transaction. No provision is made for transfer of funds electronically from an individual account holder to the retailer's account. Therefore, this is a billing procedure only, with each customer billed at the end of the month by the bank as previously practiced by the retailer. Nevertheless, no paper will pass between the store and the bank. This constitutes an initial step in the evolution of the system which we describe.

As more computing capacity becomes available, the bank will seek to tie more retailers into the system and offer the identification cards to all of its demand deposit account holders. Provision may be made for electronic transactions between retailer and customer. Eventually, it is hoped that transactions between customers holding accounts in different banks could be made by establishing on-line connections between banks.

The heart of the present system is a central information file which stores account information about each bank customer in such a way that the status of any account can be determined almost immediately. The central information file has in storage (1) a CIF record that contains a customer's name and the number of his various accounts and (2) a set of records, one for each type of account, which shows the balance within the account and includes a cross-reference to the customer's name. In operation, it is possible for a bank officer or teller to call into a central computer room with a customer's name and to receive in a very short time the status of any or all of the customer's accounts.

Each customer in the experiment with Storm Shoes has a special account which is tied into the CIF with a number similar to his demand deposit account number. When a purchase is made in the shoe store, the account is instantaneously updated. A verification of a previously established line of credit and credit rating of the customer's account can be made by the clerk in the shoe store before initiating the transaction. Bank officials, by means of a special dialed-in code, can ask for account balance information and for several other types of information, such as monthly average balance or date of last deposit.

In developing the equipment needed to operate the system, the bank has made ingenious use of the most modern types of data-transmission and input-output devices. Purchases made in the shoe stores, for example, are accomplished by inserting a plastic identification card, punched with holes to indicate the account number, into a touch-tone telephone equipped with a card dialer. After this initial contact with the computer is made, and the amount of the transaction, clerk number, and so on are keyed in on the touch-tone's buttons, verbal confirmation of the customer's account number and the amount of the purchase is sent back to the store by means of an audio-response unit which "generates" a voice answer from directions given it by the computer.

Even with the sophisticated equipment presently in use, a number of aspects of the system are not as automated as the bank intends them eventually to be. The clerk in the shoe store must dial up the bank, for example, in order to connect the touch-tone terminal in the store with the bank's computer. (This dial-up is automated, however, by means of a card dialer phone system.) Some of the requests from bank tellers and officers are still handled by a group of clerks who receive the call from the requestor, key a terminal device, receive a typed response from the computer, and finally relay the message by phone to the requestor.

Even the disposition of the experimental customers' accounts is not fully "automatic." Although the amount of each purchase is deducted from the customer's special account balance, the customer is either notified before the amount is deducted from his actual demand deposit account or he is billed by the bank and subsequently pays by regular check.

When sufficient experience with the system has been achieved, the bank intends to eliminate the present manual operations almost completely. Eventually, the on-line stores will have a direct connection with the bank's computer. A system will be developed for automatically verifying that a customer has sufficient funds to make a purchase. Equipment capable of checking a cardholder's identity will be acquired, and bank officers will eventually have direct access to all account records through the use of new terminal devices.

ON-LINE, REAL-TIME BANKING

On-line, real-time banking has been pioneered by savings banks and the savings and loan associations. Demonstrated equipment feasibility and economics of such operations together with the development of the central information file have given bankers in all areas of banking a potent new marketing and operational tool. A total financial services package can be provided to consumers today. Bankers are acquiring the necessary equipment for multiple access, remote station, real-time operations and are devoting systems development effort to the accomplishment of central information file capability.

Three major benefits may be noted for on-line, real-time banking:

1. Banks are able to provide faster service for their customers. In this age of convenience, the time required to service a depositor or loan applicant can be the differentiating factor that gains or loses a customer for the bank.

2. There is a reduced risk of losses on withdrawals, demand deposit debits, and consumer loans when access to account status and credit information is accomplished at the time of transaction.

3. An OLRT system is specifically designed to produce only desired information rather than all the data. Sophisticated computer installations will also be able to be used more productively in other profit producing applications.

Most banks have currently concentrated on using random-access, real-time computers to provide account status on savings and demand deposits. A smaller number of banks, unilaterally or in cooperation with credit bureaus, have also updated information from credit records "instantly." The Union Commerce Bank, Cleveland, in 1965 introduced a service to provide immediate updating and status information for its savings and checking accounts from all its offices. The Harris Trust and Savings Bank, Chicago, introduced a similar service to provide on-line savings and mortgage loan accounting for both its own customers and those of outside subscribing institutions.

For credit information, the Bank of America under a cooperative agreement with Credit Data Corporation (CDC) is able to obtain a credit check on every new loan application within 90 seconds. The agreement also provides for the updating of credit information. CDC has nearly 350 subscribers, including five other banks, and has credit histories of five million persons presently in storage. This arrangement has enabled Bank of America to reduce its credit-check costs by 25-50 percent. In another use of credit data, Texas Bank and Trust Company, Dallas, is employing a random access computer to provide instant credit information for 700 participating merchants in connection with its Texas Bank Charge-It Cards. These institutions are representative of the many that are now operating on-line in real-time. However, of much greater significance is the high proportion of banks reporting that they have ordered the necessary computers and peripheral access equipment and are planning for OLRT operations between 1967 and 1970.

One of the critical components of an OLRT cash and credit system is a random-access central information file (CIF). For the banks adopting OLRT capability, this requires the construction of a consolidated file of all information concerning each present or potential customer of the bank. The early construction of such a file has significant advantages, even if the CIF precedes by only a few years a completely integrated OLRT cash and credit system. The CIF eliminates duplications and inconsistencies resulting from separate files. It permits examination of the total relationship the customer has with his bank. It enables the bank to improve its marketing effort by identifying which customers, present or prospective, are not using the bank's services and where they are located. Together with credit data on each customer, either developed internally or obtained from external sources, the bank can use the central information file to organize and direct its planning programs to serve its community and maximize its profits.

The Bank of Delaware, in the venture discussed earlier, pioneered in the development of such a central information file. The bank's installation, as with any OLRT banking system, hinges upon the CIF as the basic element which can then be combined with economic and statistical data to build an information utility computerizing the bank's range of client services. Such an internal system, based on the CIF, can ultimately be expanded into a fully integrated OLRT cash and credit system, linked with other banks, many retail outlets, and eventually with private telephones throughout the community.

In conclusion, we see that access and processing speeds for random-access computers have increased enormously over the past few years. Further significant efficiencies in the near future are promised by all the major EDP equipment manufacturers. Simultaneously, the costs of mass storage are decreasing just as dramatically. Computer manufacturers and peripheral equipment suppliers are also offering remote input/output devices for a variety of functions at ever lower costs. On-line, real-time banking is today economically feasible and strategically important in preparation for tomorrow's opportunities.

Development of central information files, sophisticated marketing techniques, and OLRT capability places the progressive bank on the threshold of an electronic cash and credit system. Services and profits will increase. Surveys of progressive banks indicate that, with little differentiation because of size, equipment-buying plans and systems designs favor the emergence of an on-line, real-time system. The electronic cash and credit system complements the trend to convenience in an industry where service makes the difference, and banking leaders are moving to make this possible.

CHAPTER V

THE CREDIT SECTOR •

T HIS CHAPTER will discuss how and why large numbers of credit-granting institutions and credit-reporting institutions will ultimately be integrated with an OLRT electronic transfer system. The general functions, trends, and types of consumer credit will be examined, and we will discuss the functions and practices of the credit-reporting industry. Significant problems facing this industry will be briefly outlined along with trends and innovational changes occurring within the sector. The discussion will then focus on the development of computerized credit information files and some of the problems related to this development. A final section will analyze the credit granting institutions.

GROWTH OF CONSUMER CREDIT

Definition and scope of consumer credit. "Consumer credit" may be defined as personal loans or credits granted consumers to be used for financing purchases of consumer goods and services. This practice, developed in the 1920's, grew dynamically after World War II and has placed a significant role domestically in the development, maintenance, and expansion of markets for consumer durable goods. In recent years, consumer credit has also helped significantly to develop and expand the market for nondurable goods and services.

The time dimension involved in consumer credit ranges from short-term charge account credit services of 30 days to long-term real estate mortgage credit extended over a period of years. By using consumer credit, people who have been unable to accumulate capital in advance for the purchase of goods have been able to enjoy these goods while meeting monthly payments convenient for their budgets. Thus consumer credit has become one of our most important means of financing the flow of goods and services.

To provide consumer credit, an elaborate and complex structure of special credit-reporting organizations and credit-granting or financial institutions has developed. The growth of this structure has paralleled the dramatic growth of credit in the postwar years. We have witnessed, since 1945, an expansion of installment and noninstallment consumer credit from $6 billion to $76 billion. Installment credit alone has increased from about $3 billion to $60 billion. To put it in different terms, American consumers today have committed over 14 percent of their disposable income to meet the obligations of their installment agreements. With estimates that disposable income between 1966 and 1970 might grow by 30 percent and with the additional expectation that a larger portion of this disposable income will be available for discretionary purchases (purchases of commodities which are most usually associated with the use of consumer installment credit), the magnitude of consumer credit can be expected to continue growing dynamically in the future. Tomorrow's economy should also provide a general environment where credit risks are reduced, credit coverage is broader, and the number and variety of credit grantors are greater. Some experts feel that by 1970 consumer lending will be at least 50 percent higher than the level attained in 1965.

Another trend directly related to consumer credit is the shift in the age distribution of the population toward youth and the accompanying income redistribution. Over half of the American consuming public will soon be under the age of 25. By 1970, there will probably be over 100 million consumers in this category. By 1980, this number may approach 150 million. Because the young have not generated sufficient capital to keep up with their consumption requirements, this sector tends to be a net borrower, eager to live off available consumer credit in anticipation of larger future earnings. Also, as this segment continues to become more affluent, expectations of future earning ability rise even more, with the result that the youth sector can be expected to provide an increasingly more important market for consumer credit.

Types of consumer credit. The major types of consumer credit are installment credit and noninstallment credit. Installment credit represents credit that is scheduled for repayment in two or more payments. Thus revolving-credit, budget, and coupon accounts are treated as installment credit, since they provide for a scheduled repayment. In 1965, the largest subdivision within the installment credit category was automobile paper, amounting to over 40 percent of this type of credit issued. Personal loans and other consumer-goods paper each make up slightly less than 30 percent. The remainder is absorbed by repair and modernization loans. Noninstallment credit absorbs less than 25 percent of total consumer credit and is divided into single payment loans, charge accounts, and service credit.

Financial institutions. Financial institutions hold over 90 percent of all consumer installment credit outstanding in 1965. These firms can be divided into three categories: commercial banks, accounting for more than 40 percent of all holdings; sales finance companies, which account for about 30 percent; and other financial institutions, which account for the balance. The role of banks in consumer credit was discussed in the previous chapter.

Sales finance companies are engaged chiefly in the purchase of installment paper that arises from sales of durable consumer goods.

Other financial institutions include credit unions, consumer finance companies, mutual savings banks, and savings and loan associations. Credit unions and consumer finance companies absorb over 90 percent of the credit holdings of these other institutions. Seventy percent is personal loans, 20 percent automobile paper, and the balance is other paper and loans. In the noninstallment credit area, commercial banks and retail outlets absorb over two-thirds of these holdings.

Recent developments in noninstallment credit have changed and broadened this service. Since 1956, credit card accounts have more than doubled their credit holdings. Nevertheless, they still absorb only a small portion of noninstallment credit. Service credit, the amount owed by individuals to professional practitioners and service establishments, also has more than doubled in the 1955-1965 period. In 1963 service credit accounted for more than 25 percent of total noninstallment credit.

Implications for an OLRT transfer system. Certain conclusions can be drawn relevant to our study of future markets for OLRT systems. First, credit has grown rapidly and will continue to grow in the decade through 1976. Secondly, the increasing diversity of credit grantors may continue so that a more elaborate structure of financial and service organizations may develop to provide credit. Third, dynamic changes, occurring within this structure, are adding to its complexity. The advent of credit cards and service credit are two examples. Finally, environmental and economic trends toward increases in consumer disposable income and changes in the distribution of this income will mean that society's credit needs will become broader and more complex in the future.

One major obstacle restricting the development of an OLRT credit transfer system is the relatively low level of sophistication of many credit grantors. Small merchants grant credit to remain competitive with larger department stores. Thus they often form their own credit bureaus to serve their particular needs. Hence a proliferation of small, unsophisticated, and unscientific credit information bureaus and credit-analyzing services has emerged.

Credit grantors base credit decisions on a wide variety of evaluative criteria creating a need for unique, specialized, central-file information. The net result is that bank credit information files, sales financing files, building-material dealer files, installment credit files, and many other types of files have only segregated consumer information into smaller pieces rather than integrating information into more economical all-purpose central files.

An on-line, real-time system will appeal primarily to credit grantors that are willing and able to use scientific techniques in making their credit decisions. Today several grantors are pioneering the use of these scientific techniques, and we predict that by 1985 there will be a major change from credit management as an art to credit management as a science.

THE CREDIT-REPORTING INDUSTRY

As a result of the dynamic growth of credit purchasing, credit grantors are depending more and more on outside sources for pertinent information on their credit subjects. Experts have estimated that in 1965, 100-150 million nonduplicated credit inquiries were being made per year in the U.S. This already large number of inquiries may be increasing by as much as 10 percent per year for the country as a whole. For example, for the first nine months of 1965 the number of credit reports made by members of the Associated Credit Bureaus of America was 12 percent above the number made in the corresponding nine months of 1964. As the demand for credit information has expanded, so have the number of service organizations reporting credit information. This development in credit-reporting services has been largely characterized by a fragmented and segregated growth pattern, with the result that large numbers of small credit-reporting organizations are scattered throughout the country. In some metropolitan communities, for example, there may be as many as 25 credit bureaus or credit reporting organizations.

Services offered by credit bureaus. The typical credit bureau until recently has remained a largely passive organization. That is, it accepts information on consumers, stores it, and sells the information to subscribers with little or no analysis or processing of the information. Decisions on granting credit are usually made by the subscribers themselves, applying their own unique decision rules to the basic historical data supplied by the bureau. No financial responsibility or credit risk is taken by the bureau.

There is a large variety of credit-reporting organizations. Some are large, national or international in scope, and provide file reports or reference books to subscribers. One example of a large agency is Dun and Bradstreet. Other organizations are more restricted in the scope of their operations and provide specialized information to a particular trade or industry. An example of such an organization is the Lyon Furniture Mercantile Agency. However, by far the largest number of credit-reporting organizations are local credit bureaus which are territorially restricted agencies. During the last few years, a number of organizations have been formed to provide new services, such as check-cashing information. These services, to be discussed in more detail later, provide protection from fraud, and information and assurance to merchants cashing checks.

The information provided by subscribers to credit bureaus encompasses a wide range of data. The majority of bureaus collect and accumulate information on some or all of these items: name, address, previous address, employment, previous employment, length of service, spouse's name, standing debts, length account has been active, amount of loan or credit, terms and delinquency standing, name of bank, number of children, telephone number, regular income, purpose of loan or credit, personal references, car owner, telephone owner, life insurance owner, home owner, other income, legal judgments, nearest relatives, criminal offenses. At the same time, there are a large number of reports that can vary considerably in length and type which credit bureaus provide subscribers. These reports vary from the provision of simple derogatory information to the provision of all of the information in a subject's file. Within this range, there are probably 14 or more report categories that credit bureaus provide their subscribers. Though no single bureau may provide all of these categories, many provide a substantial portion of them. The fee charged by credit bureaus for these reports range from only a few pennies per inquiry to $3.00 or more per inquiry.

There are also different techniques by which credit bureaus receive and provide information to subscribers. These techniques range from telephone calls, with fairly immediate response, to mail response, involving a delay of from one to three days. The technique used is determined by the time constraints facing the subscriber. While some subscribers need instant response, others can afford to wait. Generally speaking, large retail stores or department stores need fast credit-inquiry and response service. On the other hand, a petroleum company needing information for its credit card accounts may have little need for such fast service.

Problems faced by credit bureaus. There are many problems in meeting retailers' information needs with available services. For example, a credit bureau will keep every last bit of information that might conceivably have a bearing on one's credit standing. Sometimes subscribers pay large sums for credit reports varying in length from a simple "no information" report to a very lengthy multipage report which includes photostatic copies of news items, photographs, and other nondigital information. In addition, some credit bureau subscribers have complained about the lack of cooperation on the part of the credit bureau in supplying information promptly. Credit bureaus are equally vocal in articulating a lack of cooperation on the part of credit grantors in promptly supplying updated source information.

Another significant problem facing subscribers of credit-reporting organizations is the fact that the cost of their credit-granting operations is very high because of the expenses of preventing and absorbing charge and installment loan delinquencies. Much of the procedural cost of acquiring an installment loan is the cost of credit reports supplied by outside reporting organizations. A credit grantor, for example, often has to make several inquiries to different reporting organizations in order to obtain sufficient information on his subject.

Different reporting organizations also experience extensive duplication in the collection and storage of information. Data collected by one organization are often unknown to others who could make good use of them. Jurisdictional, mechanical, procedural, and geographical constraints often prevent the efficient sharing of information among various organizations. Because of a high population mobility, information on the same subject may appear in the files of large numbers of credit reporting agencies. An example of this duplication can be found in the police information network (PIN) of a nine-county area around San Francisco Bay. There were some 14 million subject records in the files of just 12 of the agencies involved in PIN, although the total population of these nine counties was about four million.* Furthermore, inadequate credit investigation procedures and faulty credit reports are causing unsound decisions, with the result

* "Small Cities and Time Sharing," *Public Automation,* June 1965.

that many installment loans eventually develop into problem accounts and potential losses. These problem accounts could be eliminated at the outset by effective evaluation of risks while such loans are still in the acquisition stage. Improvement in the general quality of a credit file will reduce considerably the risks connected with costly problem accounts.

These problems and complaints on the part of credit bureau subscribers are not surprising when one remembers that credit bureaus are information suppliers or passive service organizations reacting to the needs of retailers. Since credit bureaus are in many cases formed or owned by retail stores and since they are often undercapitalized, their passive role and inability to overcome these problems are certainly not unusual. For example, generally negative reactions are typical from credit bureaus when considering the development of OLRT capability to service the kind of system we propose. Credit bureaus researched in many cities by the firm of Touche, Ross, Bailey & Smart (in a report prepared for Sperry Utah) indicated a rather uninterested and negative reaction when queried about participation in the OLRT system concept.

While probably a large number of credit bureaus will remain passive and will fail to provide more satisfactory service to credit grantors, a few credit bureaus have recognized the need for change, have upgraded and improved their services, and are viewing OLRT system participation with a more positive attitude. Several believe, as do the authors, that future survival of the credit bureaus will at some date in the near future depend on the bureaus linking up with the community OLRT cash and credit system. The Pittsburgh Credit Bureau, one of the most progressive bureaus in the country, is in the process of automating its account-numbering system. In the long term, Pittsburgh foresees the need and is developing the capability to link up with an OLRT system.

Innovations by credit bureaus. Since it is likely that only the more progressive credit-reporting organizations will be initially receptive and favorably disposed to linking up with an OLRT system, it is worthwhile mentioning some of the innovations these progressive services are adopting. The innovations are significant because they are providing both the experience and the education which is crucial to the future development of an integrated OLRT system that provides more useful and immediate credit information to a large number of credit grantors. These innovations are an immediate and necessary step in the evolution toward an OLRT system.

One of the most significant innovations in the credit-reporting industry is the development of increasingly more sophisticated *credit-scoring systems.* Credit evaluation today is still largely an art involving time-consuming and expensive human judgment. Because credit information is highly fragmented, costly, and often impossible to obtain in complete form, many progressive credit grantors are viewing credit scoring as a technique for reducing credit investigation costs and minimizing bad debt losses. In simple form, credit scoring is used to determine whether immediate purchasing privileges are to be granted to new credit applicants according to standardized, objective criteria. These techniques serve to reduce greatly the cost and time necessary for processing the data coming from the local credit bureaus. As credit-scoring techniques become more sophisticated, the credit manager is able to become more and more objective in assessing degrees of risk involved in given applications. Also, credit investigators can develop consistency when differentiating between good and bad risks. Some highly sophisticated scoring systems, employing advanced mathematical techniques as well as the use of computers, are providing more than just guidelines for making credit decisions. These systems actually make decisions about whether to approve or reject a subject on the basis of the criteria established by the designer of the credit-scoring system. Credit bureaus capable of applying the scoring techniques themselves to the data in their files are thus able to supply credit grantors with objective ratings rather than simple "file dumps" of all the data collected by the bureau. Thus the entire function of credit analysis can be, and is being, conducted by the more progressive credit bureaus through the application of sophisticated scoring techniques, most of which lend themselves to computerization and OLRT inquiry service capability.

Limited experience to date indicates that investments in simple scoring systems have resulted in considerable savings. For one personal finance company, it was estimated that objective scoring reduced bad debt losses by as much as 30 percent, and delinquent accounts were reduced by as much as 33 percent. Credit bureau expenses for another large organization have been reduced by over 25 percent through the use of a scoring system. General Electric Credit Corporation (GECC), a firm that has pioneered the credit-scoring concept, has instituted test credit-scoring programs throughout the country and currently has about 35 different scoring systems in operation. The problem of accounting for different regional consumer characteristics can be resolved, it is felt, by the introduction of 15 to 20 variations in the scoring system. GECC is enthusiastic about the effect of credit scoring on the future profitability of its company. This system not only reduces its information collection and information processing costs but also provides GECC an opportunity to serve its dealers better. The wealth of information that computers are able to process helps GECC predict problems for individual offices, thus allowing preventive actions in advance. Since credit-scoring techniques can reduce complex data on individual subjects to a numerical or digital evaluation scale, we believe the use of these techniques is essential for organizations wishing to realize the economies offered by participation within an OLRT system's network.

A second innovation in the credit-reporting industry is the use of *on-line computers for the processing of credit information*. While most of such computer applications now employ batch-processing techniques for information handling, this innovation of on-line computer access in credit reporting is a major step in the ultimate development of an OLRT system. The technique of batch processing does not provide the instant access and retrieval of information which would be possible in a real-time configuration.

Pioneering in the application of on-line credit information systems is the Hooper-Holmes Bureau Inc., Morristown, New Jersey. The mail order industry in 1964 incurred a $20 million bad-debt loss. Since the incidence of mail order fraud and other bad-debt activity was rising and since traditional credit-reporting methods provided by credit bureaus and other organizations were unable to provide rapid, appropriate, inexpensive information, the need for an automated low-cost system developed. To fill this need, Hooper-Holmes developed a systems configuration employing both high-speed data processing equipment and special on-line communications facilities. Their service provides for transmission of credit information on customers by telephone from distant collection points directly to the firm's data processing center. At this center, information is automatically screened by a computer, and the results are returned to the inquiring company within 24 hours. The service has been formed to provide direct mail merchandisers (for example, book-of-the-month clubs, record-of-the-month clubs) with a more efficient and scientific method of checking the status of prospective customers than previously was possible. Hooper-Holmes does not anticipate switching to a real-time capability in the near future. Instant information access and response are not needed by the majority of its subscribers, who can easily wait one day or so until their inquiry "batch" is run.

A third innovation paving the way for OLRT application to the credit-reporting industry is the recent development of *automated check-cashing information services* that provide protection from fraud, plus information and assurance to subscribers who cash checks for customers. Examples of this service are Credit Data Corporation and Telecredit of California. The system configuration employed by such organizations, however, is usually designed with both on-line and real-time capability. The major innovation employed by Telecredit Inc. is an on-line, real-time information retrieval system. This device, employing an IBM-305 RAMAC system, allows bank tellers, supermarket clerks, or other on-line merchants to verify a customers check-cashing status instantly.

These services are being developed independently as well as in conjunction with progressive credit bureaus throughout the country and represent another significant step in the evolutionary process toward a more integrated OLRT information facility. Several of these service organizations have plans to broaden their coverage so that more retail participants and a greater number of communities can be serviced more efficiently. Credit Data Corporation, for example, has a long-range goal of opening information centers which will be electronically linked by one network to many major population areas of the nation. It is also interesting to note that these services are being developed with the cooperation and active participation of other institutions within a regional community. The "Indy-check" service developed by Indianapolis to reduce the bad-debt losses resulting from the passing of bad checks has enlisted the cooperation of major Indianapolis banks, the police department, the Marion County sheriff's department, the Indiana state police, the FBI, and the Merchant Association for the Supply of Derogatory Information. Continual cooperation among different institutions, both public and private, within a community or region will be critical for the development of more sophisticated, broader, and comprehensive OLRT credit information systems. Hopefully, this modest institutional cooperation that has paved the way for these pilot or embryonic integrated information files will provide an example for the larger institutions that eventually must cooperate if a viable OLRT cash and credit transfer and information system is to become a reality.

Recently, a joint development program has been launched by IBM and the Associated Credit Bureaus of America for studying the automation of credit bureaus. The conclusion of this study calls for a systems configuration very similar in concept to the ones described earlier. Some of the characteristics of their proposed credit information system include: record location in less than one second, a memory capability up to 400 million characters per data cell to provide information on as many as two million subjects, and a large direct access synonym dictionary to serve as a cross-reference file to provide more positive identification.

The constraining problems for continued rapid innovation in this field appear not to lie in the area of technological or economic constraints. Rather, the major constraints at this time appear to be the various social and political factors which are, quite expectedly, inhibiting rapid changes.

National finance and loan companies. National finance and loan companies have been taking an increasingly active role in providing consumer credit. The rapid expansion of consumer credit for automobile and other consumer durable goods purchasing (as well as the unsatisfactory credit-reporting services provided by some credit bureaus) has resulted in the evolution of special companies like General Motors Acceptance Corporation, General Electric Credit Corporation, CIT, and Commercial Credit Corporation. In the area of real estate and home improvement credit, a similar development has occurred with the advent of Household Finance Corporation.

The services offered by these organizations have evolved for two main reasons. First, commercial banks were leaving a vacuum in the lower-income sector of the consumer loan and credit market. Therefore, needs for credit and loans in this sector were not being satisfied. Secondly, the traditional outlets for providing credit information were often providing poor quality and costly reporting. To overcome these weaknesses, the new organizations attempted to rationalize and strengthen their own credit-information processing. As these organizations have expanded, their services have grown to include consumer-budgeting arrangements. It seems entirely probable that instant loans and instant credit might be new services which would appeal to finance companies.

Personal-budgeting help and automatic credit and loan services would allow finance organizations to establish stronger relationships with their present clients, while at the same time allowing these organizations to reach even more toward servicing the lower end of the consumer credit and loan market. This segment is a large relatively untapped market for consumer credit. When the standard of living of the lower fifth of the American population rises, as it certainly will within the next ten or fifteen years, this market sector will provide attractive opportunities for consumer credit.

Although the types of information on consumers that financial organizations require for granting loans vary, many of the data needed for credit loans are very similar to the data which will be required by other integrated OLRT system participants. OLRT inquiry devices could service credit grantors with customer information of the credit bureau type but with perhaps more thorough (and expensive) credit-scoring analysis. As computerized credit analysis services become established and are on-line to the finance companies, finance companies will be less exposed to risks. Use of more sophisticated decision rules and computerized files will enable them to store and process more complete and more accurate data on customers.

There are several indications that these credit and loan organizations are moving into more scientific management techniques and thus are paving their way for eventual participation within an integrated OLRT system. As previously discussed, GECC has been experimenting for a number of years with credit-scoring techniques. After an effective and comprehensive credit-scoring system becomes a reality for GECC, its transition to OLRT link-up should be rapid.

Another recent development in this industry has been the computerization of reporting by Household Finance Corporation. In the middle of 1965, HFC announced that it would install a $10-million IBM network to connect more than 1,000 branch offices with two computers in Chicago for record-keeping and reporting purposes. When completely operational, the system will handle an average of more than 150,000 transactions daily. This configuration will involve peripheral equipment, direct communication's linkup, and instant information response and retrieval. The central memory files will hold complete records on two million customers and the service is projected to begin operation in 1967. This innovation, probably representative of the direction that other progressive national finance and loan companies are following, will assist in the development of community and regional OLRT systems technology.

It appears, therefore, that national finance and loan companies will be important elements of an integrated electronic cash and credit system. Their willingness to accept increased risk at higher interest rates and to service a growing market segment places them in an important role as a credit grantor. Developments of high-speed information storage and transmission capability will serve to support this role as an effective and profitable OLRT participant.

National credit and travel companies. The second category includes the national credit and travel companies. Other organizations now operating within the ancillary credit field which are potential integrated-systems participants would include American Express, Diners' Club, Carte Blanche, national car rental agencies, national gasoline companies, airlines, motels and hotels, travel agents, railroads, shipping lines, and national restaurant chains.

The concept of national OLRT service facilitating relatively positive and instant credit authorization, reservations acceptance, credit purchasing, and centralized customer billing would make credit traveling available to a much larger number of people with far less exposure to risks than is presently being experienced. This service also lends itself well to integration at point of origin with other communications equipment and systems used by other subscribers. According to Touche, Ross, Bailey & Smart, a study of a single reservation-charge-billing system for Carte Blanche, Sheraton, Diners' Club, and American Express showed that an OLRT system could be justified. These organizations were found to have national credit images, national marketing facilities, and as business entities, the availability of capital resources for expansion. Thus, unlike many local credit bureaus, these firms can be expected to promote actively and exploit the credit industry.

In the past, many organizations providing credit card services have had a number of abortive undertakings which have given these organizations at times an undesirable image. A major problem facing this industry today is related to the credit card. Cards are lost too frequently, and necessary reissue is expensive. Often individuals will carry a number of charge cards and thus can bargain for credit service when derogatory information has frozen the use of one card. Stealing of credit cards has been increasing. For example, dollar losses from the misuse of credit cards have increased eight times in the 1958-1962 period, to a level of approximately $2 billion. In 1964, approximately 2 percent of the credit cards in circulation were lost. Of those that were lost 4 percent, or approximately 60,000 were stolen. It is estimated that illicit charges on a stolen card average $500. Thus significant improvement will be necessary in developing a foolproof security card and system of identification before OLRT systems using a universal credit card can develop rapidly.

We are witnessing today a number of moves by national credit card organizations and bank credit cards to expand and increase their services. Most credit card companies are expanding greatly the number and variety of subscribing merchants who will honor their cards. National credit cards can now be used for food, clothes, drink, entertainment, travel, accommodations—for almost anything one might want to buy. Even traveler's checks or a cash bond can be obtained on some credit cards. As many of the larger credit card companies expand their services, the differentiating advantages of holding one card over another tend to decrease rather than increase. The logical extension of the current trends will be a number of universally accepted credit cards. The next step is to make each card machine-readable and to effect card changes through OLRT equipment.

The final step is the adoption of the one universal card, reducing the present national credit card companies to national credit companies, with each company using essentially the same card.

Therefore, alternatives that may evolve for these credit card companies are:

1. Merge with banks and integrate the card into the one, universal card required of an electronic transfer system.
2. Merge with each other to form one large organization granting credit. This alternative may eventually lead to merging with a bank system to provide cards that may be used universally.
3. Supply credit information as a credit bureau type of service. In addition, credit card companies might supply higher-risk credit in competition with other financial institutions.
4. Expand credit services overseas to take advantage of growing credit requirements and an apparent lag in adoption of an OLRT electronic transfer system.

OLRT CREDIT IN THE FUTURE

Evolution toward OLRT will most likely occur first on a regional rather than a national level. Regional sponsors such as credit bureaus will play a major role in this evolution. These credit bureaus will begin to fulfill this role as they improve the quality of their information reporting. Automation and mechanization through computer-based systems, as well as the development of standardized scoring system, will provide great improvements in their reporting services capability. By providing complete, factual, and inexpensive information to subscribers, credit bureaus will be an important element in a fully integrated OLRT cash and credit network. Many on-line information subscribers will want to purchase complete OLRT credit analysis services, applying credit-scoring and decision-making rules to assist them in their credit granting. The most progressive credit bureaus will be able to supply such information on-line and in real-time. The survival of those credit bureaus which fail to improve their services through the use of modern hardware and software systems will be seriously threatened. A large number of the smaller organizations can be expected to cease business operations as other more capable credit grantors and reporting services take over a large portion of their traditional business.

CHAPTER VI

RETAILING •

T HE RETAIL STORE'S point of sale has already been described as being a vital link in the proposed OLRT funds transfer system. It is here that transaction inputs to the system originate. It is here that the customer has his primary contact with the electronic network that serves him. The retail store, placed on-line to a central computer system, provides the crucial link between the customer and his source of funds, and triggers the transaction process.

Because his participation is so vital to the system, it is essential to win the acceptance, support, and cooperation of the retail merchant and to convince him of the advantages of OLRT participation as an aid to his own operations. In this chapter, we seek to outline to the retailer the merits of our proposal from his point of view. We seek his endorsement of an enthusiastic participation in an electronic cash and credit system.

CUSTOMER SERVICE AND CONVENIENCE

Dynamic changes in retailing since World War II have accented the need for continued management attention to customer service. Population growth, the movement of population to the suburbs, increasing affluence, and a proliferation of new products have forced retailing management to evaluate constantly its attention to customer services.

Granting of retail credit has been one of the major areas of service demanded by retailer customers in recent years. Competitive pressures have forced most retailers to offer their customers credit. The customer has come to view retail credit as an expected convenience service.

In recent years, even discounters have been forced by competitive pressures to begin offering customer-credit services. This response to customer demands and competitive pressures is significant when one considers that discount operations, as a rule, were generally established on the premise of providing only minimal customer service with the compensating advantage of lower prices. The widespread introduction of charge plans by discounters within the past decade dramatically underscores the importance of offering retail credit privileges to today's demanding customer.

Department store credit transactions often average 60 percent of sales volume. We note a historical trend away from the use of cash as a trading medium in today's transaction system. This use of credit cards, instead of cash, for daily retail transactions is an important step in paving the way for OLRT transactions, in that customers are naturally becoming accustomed to the kind of system whereby virtually all currency as a medium of retail exchange will be eliminated.

This trend away from the use of cash is all the more apparent when one considers the vast amount of other products and services now offered for credit, such as transportation, fuel, restaurant meals, lodging, and so on.

Although the existence of credit services provides the individual customer with the benefit of carrying little cash, some inconvenience is inherent in the present system of credit granting and reporting. A customer must establish credit in each store where he wishes to trade. This involves a credit interview or application requiring a consumer to answer a battery of the same kind of questions for each store. If a customer is deemed an unacceptable credit risk, rejection may cause embarrassment to both retailer and consumer. In either case, there is the delay occasioned by the store's reference to a central credit bureau. In case of a satisfactory check from the credit bureau, a charge card is issued, often with a delay of many days if not a few weeks. In the meantime, the store might issue temporary limited-purchase cards, but the net effect of the process likely means bothersome delay for the customer and lost sales potential for the retailer. Even with established store credit, there is often delay at the point of sale, while the sales clerk makes a credit check with the store's office. Finally, at the end of an accounting period, a customer receives bills from each of the several stores where he has traded and has to make separate payment to each.

An OLRT transactions system offers the consumer convenience and services not possible under our present credit and transaction mechanisms.

Central credit information files will eliminate the need for multiple credit interviews at each store. Consistent and current information will be available to each retailer instantly upon inquiry. Electronic transactions at the point of sale will be greatly expedited, adding convenience to the consumer's retail shopping experience. With the advent of the central OLRT credit system, one master statement listing all the accounting period's transactions will be sent monthly to the customer. Since each of the transactions listed represents a payment made to a retailer (not a debt owed to a retailer), the ritual of writing monthly checks to pay bills will be completely eliminated. His bank credit has automatically paid his bills at time of transaction; consolidated "bill payment" then takes place automatically as the bank credit is liquidated (by an automatic deposit of payroll funds to the customer's account, for example).

The current use of bank credit cards is an important initial step toward electronically linking banks and retailers in a centralized information and transaction system. In a 1963 market study (conducted by Harlan R. Patterson for a Michigan State University doctoral dissertation), "convenience" was the prime reason expressed by consumers for using bank charge services. Women used the card more than men and noted that "the ability to use credit at a variety of stores by using only one credit card" was the most desired "convenience." Certainly, an extension of the well-received bank card concept to a fully integrated electronic system will add much more to the convenience package retailers are seeking to provide.

ADVANTAGES TO THE RETAILER

Retail establishments vary in size and volume of transactions from the small, neighborhood, independently owned store to large chains and department stores. Economies of scale permit larger stores to place great emphasis on satisfying customer demands through improved, and sometimes expensive, services, such as credit. As a result, many of the small retailers have been unable to compete satisfactorily with larger stores in carrying these expensive credit services or using automated data processing equipment. An indication of what this is meaning over the long run to the smaller retailers is illustrated by the historical net reduction of 1 percent in total retail establishments in the 1955-1965 period while total dollar expenditures for retail goods have increased about 5 percent each year. Although it is not likely that many small retailers have been driven out of business because of the added expense of offering their own credit plans, it is likely that many who have not offered credit have lost customers and sales to stores which have been able to provide these services.

The OLRT network will give all the benefits of economies of scale to any on-line participant, regardless of size. OLRT systems should have a significant impact on the competitiveness of smaller retailers, since credit service for customers, and EDP control services to assist management, will be available on-line. Small retailers participating in community bank charge plans already attest to increased business because of improved services made possible with a centralized card. This phenomenon should also serve to illustrate that initial converts to an OLRT cash and credit system will probably be those who have the most to gain through participation. Once some merchants in a community participate, however, their competitive edge will induce the remainder of the community's merchants to come on-line with a subsequent universal subscription to the system's services.

Many large stores will find an OLRT transfer system a welcome relief from the burden of operating their own credit system. With on-line credit services available to their customers, expensive efforts to duplicate these services with store-sponsored credit will disappear. A study by the National Retail Merchants Association indicates that even the larger-volume merchants may have difficulty in operating credit operations as efficiently as those that bankers are offering through their bank card plans. Banks are now operating their credit card business with charges to the merchant ranging from 3-7 percent of sales. They also charge the card holder up to 1.5 percent of the unpaid balance monthly. Expanded, fully computerized operations might permit these charges to be considerably reduced. Corresponding costs for store-sponsored credit services are similar for even efficient retailers. It is doubtful whether small or even medium-size merchants can perform this service as cheaply.

The inherent attraction of turning the whole credit operation over to the banks is gathering considerable appeal among many retailers. Participation in the OLRT transfer system would provide cost advantages to most, if not all, retailers because of the larger scale and efficiency of the automated system.

Another advantage that will accrue to large and small merchants alike will be to greatly decrease working capital requirements. With credit-granting activities conducted by banking or financial institutions and with instantaneous funds transfer, the burden of supporting large accounts receivable will no longer be carried by the retailer. Accounts receivable require capital in the range of 15-20 percent of annual sales for an average retailer. Funds thus released could be made available for other, more profitable, retailing investment. Likewise, the requirements for till reserves and the amount of cash "in process" as payments are received would approach zero as OLRT does away with both cash and manual payment processing. In many stores a capital base of 2 percent of annual sales is now deployed to meet these two requirements. An OLRT system would eliminate this need.

Many will argue against the OLRT proposal by insisting that customers will prefer the existing charge-bill-wait-pay cycle to any kind of system that requires instant funds transfer or credit carrying charges commencing at the instant of charge. They state a preference for the normal 30 days billing date. (Department store accounts have an average age, at present, of some 60 days before they are paid.) However, a number of features inherent in the electronic cash and credit mechanism serve to overcome this objection. In the first place, the system could easily be programmed to provide not only additional charges for credit extension but perhaps a discount for funds transfer at the time of purchase or before some established normal charge period such as 30 days. Any payment introduced to the system prior to the 30 days would give the customer an automatic prorated discount. Payment at the 30-day mark would amount to par, with no premium charge for interest and no discount for prepayment. Balances extending beyond 30 days could then be automatically charged a carrying cost, prorated on a daily basis. The net effect would be to put all funds transactions on a time-value basis with rewards for promptness and penalties for tardiness. Account holders who today pay at point of sale would receive the discount they deserve, paying some 60 days ahead of average. The greater equity of employing the time-value-of-money concept to cash and credit transactions should more than offset the objections of the few who will no longer be given a free credit ride at the expense of the prompt payers.

In our discussion thus far, we have suggested that the customer's source of credit funds would in all likelihood be an on-line commercial bank. An overdraft loan service would be closely tied to the customer's demand deposit account. Today's bank credit cards and the various overdraft "automatic loan" credit-line plans now offered by many banks are elementary beginnings to the universal bank credit card concept which we propose.

Other on-line sources of credit will service customers who wish to make purchases in excess of their existing bank credit line. These sources might include the retailer himself, who could take the option of extending credit, probably at higher interest rates than the bank's credit, for higher-risk loans. Repayment of these loans extended by the retailer (or by ancillary credit-granting institutions) could then be accomplished through automatic, prearranged installments which would periodically shift funds from the customer's demand deposit account to the account of the lender.

RETAILING MANAGEMENT WITH AN OLRT SYSTEM

Retailing institutions have been generally slow in adapting the tools of EDP to the peculiarities of marketing. Most of the delays originate with difficulties of translating unique characteristics of retailing to hardware and software combinations. Internal administrative operations, such as payroll and accounting functions, are currently using EDP techniques to assist management tasks. National Cash Register Company has recently introduced a point-of-sale system that provides logistics information which assists management in inventory decision making.

On the basis of the information triggered at point-of-sale terminals, many aspects of operations may be automatically monitored and controlled. Financial information, such as tabulations of sales volume or funds transfers, can be made instantaneously available. Inventory can be more precisely controlled through real-time stock level information and automatic reorder processing. The computer system can be designed to provide the daily sales figures, broken down by clerk, department, product, or however desired. Employees could even use the terminal device to clock in and out. The computer system could automatically and periodically compute hours, pay, deductions, and then trigger a payroll transfer to the employees' bank accounts. Compensation based wholly or in part on commissions could easily be computed, since each sale would be entered into the information system directly at point of sale.

In addition to performance of internal control and logistics information gathering, OLRT point-of-sale terminals could serve as source points for a marketing research and information system. Cashiers could key in data on the customer's age, sex, address, or planned use of a product at the same time as the transaction data is entered. A system of programs and switching computers would retain the market research information in the retailer's EDP processor while the funds transaction is completed through normal banking channels. One can readily see that the terminal device of an OLRT transfer system could serve as a source for a completely integrated management information system. Transaction data would flow through the cash and credit system; control, logistics, and market research data would be used internally for planning and decision-making purposes.

Finally, an OLRT system could remove completely the retailer's burden of operating internal credit services. Assuming a retailer exercises the option of granting his own credit in addition to the bank's, credit information about the customer available from a central computer file will greatly reduce the administrative time required of the retailer for approving and policing internal credit operations. Consequently, management can devote a more concentrated effort to the merchandising activities which it knows best and which make for more profitable retailing.

CHAPTER VII

INTERNATIONAL DEVELOPMENTS •

As ECONOMIC AND MARKETING justification becomes apparent, electronic cash and credit systems will probably evolve in other countries in a manner parallel to that in the United States. Certain features of the banking, credit, and retailing institutions in other countries are discussed in this chapter relative to the development of effective electronic transaction systems. The present state of computer and data transmission capability abroad is outlined as a basis for discussing the further electronic integration of banking, credit, and retailing institutions. An estimate of the requirements for this system is then made to lay the foundation for a prediction of future trends. Finally, the possibility of a truly integrated electronic cash and credit system across national and regional boundaries is discussed, this being the ultimate systems configuration.

BANKS

In a significant number of countries, banking assets are concentrated among a relatively small number of institutions. As a result, a banking structure has developed consisting of a small number of large banks operating extensive branch systems across a country. Canada, for example, has only eight chartered banks. The United Kingdom has about 24 joint-stock banks with a network of about 12,000 branches. On the other hand, the United States has limits placed on branch banking by various state laws. As a result, the United States has some 14,000 commercial banks with over 8,000 branch offices and approximately 22,000 banking offices.

From this, it appears that the organizational structure of a few commercial banks with a nationwide network of branches may provide an opportunity for wide geographic adoption of an electronic cash and credit system by a single banking institution, through conversion of existing central computer facilities to OLRT systems capable of serving the branches. Obviously, such a system must weigh the economics of equipment requirements for the smaller branches. Nevertheless, the basic structure of banking in other countries provides a ready framework around which an integrated system may be designed.

Industrial orientation of foreign banks. Given the concentration of assets in a few institutions, many commercial banks in other countries have historically served large businesses and international exchange customers. With their broad network of branches, these banks were ideally suited for serving industry and commerce throughout a country. While concentrating on large-account customers, however, an opportunity developed for other institutions to service smaller customers and their savings and loans accounts. As a result, in many countries a number of smaller local banks developed to serve specific needs. Savings banks, mortgage banks, and agricultural banks all derive their funds from a broad spectrum of the population and serve local customers.

Personal checks. A corollary of this development is that checks have not gained the same recognition among the general population in other countries as they have in the United States. Although businesses abroad have made ample use of checking accounts, the personal use of checks is still developing. Perhaps, therefore, with relatively little check processing in some countries and with local banking institutions serving local population needs, the present system may delay an economical conversion to an integrated electronic system in some countries. However, the credit institutions that serve the general public in a significant number of countries provide a framework for an evolving system.

CREDIT-TRANSFERRING INSTITUTIONS

Certainly, one of the unique characteristics of overseas money-movement institutions is the post giro system, or postal-check service. In most countries employing this system, the post giro system and the Post Office Savings Bank (an institution for granting interest on deposited funds) constitute the Post Office Bank. Both are under the administration of the postal system and thus have a ready-made, nationwide network.

The post giro system is a check service operated by the post office. The system provides for the transfer of payments, with or without cash, into or out of members' accounts. A formal system of forms for transferring, withdrawing, or depositing funds has been provided on a nationwide basis.

In many countries, a nonaccount holder may make payments to a giro-account holder.

The giro system of credit transfers are so effective that 40 countries in Europe, Asia, Latin America, and Africa employ this method of payment. Elements of the system which make it popular with users as well as administrators are:

1. National coverage through the mail system and post office outlets.
2. Convenience to account holders in making or receiving payments by mail or at the post office.
3. Integration of giro operation with postal system to effect operating economies.
4. Minimum charges (if any) to account holder for transactions.
5. Automatic transfers of payments for payrolls, insurance premiums, and similar repetitive transactions.

Obviously, the acceptance of this system by many countries has been a competitive threat to some commercial banks. In Sweden, for instance, the giro funds have swollen to such magnitude—about 480,000 accounts with a turnover of over 500 billion kroner ($96 billion)—that interest is paid for accounts of 50,000 kroner ($9,665) or more. As a result, several Swedish banks have formed a giro system to provide better service for their own accounts.

Adaptation of the giro system to electronics. These giro systems form a nucleus of a transfer system that could be integrated easily into a total electronic transfer system. Essentially, banking and credit transfers are wedded into one system in giro countries. In this sense, the giro mechanism is a step ahead of present American cash and credit transfer systems. With an increasing use of electronic data processing for completion of internal transfers, a logical next step would be to introduce OLRT capability and to tie in retailers to the system.

One consideration which might inhibit a giro country from adopting a totally integrated system is that, at present, cost factors for manually operated giro systems are not excessive. By association with post office services, the giro system is able to operate at very low incremental cost. Therefore, little or no charge is made to an account holder for transactions, depending on the country involved. The speed and economy with which the system presently operates may preclude a rapid need for integrating this system with the retailers through an OLRT network.

There are other credit institutions overseas that are similar to some of those appearing in the United States. These are usually of a specialized nature serving a local need, such as cooperative agricultural credit associations or mortgage banks. Possibly, these institutions might eventually be linked into a fully integrated system. However, the volume of transactions is too small, compared with the giro systems and commercial banks, to warrant early integration into the system.

RETAILERS

As in the United States, overseas merchandising establishments appear to be trailing other institutions in using the computer. But some multistore chains are now using EDP for inventory control and accounting, the pertinent information being gathered by cash-register type of equipment at the point of sale. The impetus for expanding present computer installations and developing integrated electronic transfer systems will probably not come from the retailers; the real economic incentive to promote integrated systems development will be perceived earlier by the banking institutions, especially since costly retail credit-granting systems are not generally as well established overseas as in the United States.

GOVERNMENT

The role of the governments in other countries will probably be greater in the evolution of this system than can be expected in the United States. Since many large overseas banks are chartered by their governments and since their post offices administer their giro systems, major legislation abroad may be required to permit full exploitation of fully integrated systems. On the other hand, many overseas governments are leading proponents of adopting automation techniques to make their operations more efficient. For example, in Western Europe, where employment is high and a shortage of labor exists, the governments have advocated automating the giro systems to free labor for other productive jobs.

CURRENT STATUS OF EDP AND DATA TRANSMISSION OVERSEAS

Progress in adopting EDP techniques in other countries has usually been pioneered by the U.S. computer hardware manufacturers who have built a number of systems for foreign banks and governments. Recently, many foreign organizations have been developing software to meet their specific needs and, in some cases, have innovated their own hardware-software combinations. Many of the larger banks in the industrialized countries are incorporating third-generation computer equipment with OLRT capability in their systems, and some large overseas electrical equipment and computer manufacturing firms are developing peripheral equipment (such as a terminal device for credit cards) that will assist in integrating several elements of the transfer system.

Check-handling equipment. It is interesting to note that many of the European countries adopted the CMC-7 system of magnetic characters for their checks. This system differs in reading characteristics and character style from the E13B system adopted by the United States, Canada, United Kingdom, Australia, and New Zealand. Although there are pros and cons to the merits of each system, the separate system of markings used by European countries applies to checks and therefore should not inhibit development of an integrated electronic transfer system which will eliminate paper transfer. MICR equipment is just coming into common usage overseas. Although in the United Kingdom and Canada, as well as the United States, the MICR system of document processing has been almost universally adopted, the wide variety of numbering formats in other countries which were not suited for machine processing delayed the adaptation of MICR equipment. With full standardization on the CMC-7 system of marking, however, MICR equipment should become more universally used for check processing in Europe.

Communications equipment. The quality of data transmission or telephone lines overseas may impede development of telecommunications abroad. There are significant variations in line quality among the different countries. The telephone services that can be used for transmitting data are generally not as well developed as U.S. communications networks. Also, foreign governments tightly control line allocation and maintenance of these lines. As a result, procedures for obtaining additional lines and cables may be cumbersome and time consuming.

Hole-punched checks. Significant steps have been taken in many countries to computerize the cash and credit transfer mechanisms. In Holland's post giro system, for example, the form for the postal check is a tabulating card which is prepunched with the individual's name and account number. Once the card is mailed or taken to the post office, the post giro system's computers automatically perform the desired transaction and a statement is mailed to the account holder. Significant savings are realized with computers, and the equipment is well suited for handling the increasing growth in volume of transactions that the post giro system is experiencing.

THE NEAR FUTURE

It appears likely that the evolution of electronic cash and credit systems will proceed more slowly abroad than in the United States. To date, no foreign country or installation has even experimented with a fully integrated banking, credit, and retailing network. However, the time seems ripe for further foreign developments because:

1. Equipment requirements are virtually satisfied. Terminal devices are being developed and tested. Telephone lines for data transmission are providing improved service.
2. The post giro system, used for personal credit transfers in 40 countries, provides a framework for integration of banking and credit services.
3. A tight labor market and increased volume of paper flow are incentives toward automating transfer systems to realize the economies involved.

Elements of the structure of existing institutions which will have to be resolved before integration can occur include the following:

- Post giro systems represent competition to commercial banks; these institutions will therefore have to reconcile their operations.
- Retailers will need to recognize the economic incentive to place terminals in their stores. The most industrialized countries will take the lead, since their retail market systems are more formally developed.
- Experimental systems will probably be tested in various countries. However, adoption of an integrated system will require economic justification for each institution.

Present difficulties make it unlikely that fully integrated systems will become operational in other countries by 1971. It can be expected, however, that developments in the industrialized nations abroad will lag the United States by not more than five years.

TOWARD A WORLD SYSTEM

Following the lead of the nations willing to experiment with electronic systems, neighboring countries are likely to adopt compatible systems for international funds exchange. As political and economic ties between countries become more interdependent and as communications facilities between countries improve, a natural linking of monetary transfer systems will evolve. For instance, as Common Market ties develop, the Common Market will be a likely prospect for an integrated regional system. Already, post-giro-system countries have formed an international committee that has prescribed procedures for giro transfers between giro countries. The similarity between the U.S. and Canadian economies indicates a natural opportunity for developing yet another international system. To be sure, problems such as exchange rates will have to be overcome before national transfers can become routine, but computers could accommodate exchange rate adjustments instantaneously. Another recent technological development, the communications satellite, may ultimately allow transactions to be made across very widely separated locations. This long-range possibility is less dependent on the satellite, however, than upon development of new forms of international transactions to reduce the complexities of existing methods, such as drafts and letters of credit.

CHAPTER VIII

RELATED PROBLEMS AND IMPLICATIONS •

In the evolution from today's system of funds transfers to the system which we have described, many changes in the legal aspects of banking, credit, and retail operations will occur. Some of these changes will simplify or even eliminate current problems, while other changes will present new challenges to the legal profession and to our lawmakers. Where current problems will be simplified or eliminated, the institutions involved will be able to save time and money by removing safeguards that are now deemed necessary. Or, if safeguards are not employed at this time, the risks that are now being self-insured will be reduced or eliminated.

LEGAL ASPECTS OF AN ELECTRONIC SYSTEM

In those areas where changes to existing laws or new laws will be required, attention has already been directed toward conceptualizing the broad legal framework within which the new system will operate. Legal experts from many affected sectors of the economy have been involved in this phase. From this point, the drafting of laws and amendments to laws is necessary to allow the development of specific functions of the system. Failure to take a positive approach to paving the legal road to electronic transactions could delay the application. Therefore, reduction of these concepts into specifics and timely presentation of recommendations with detailed justification and adequate support are necessary to provide for the adoption of the laws. It must be stressed that none of the problems which have been foreseen to date are considered impossible to solve. Almost certainly the solutions will occur and can be implemented before the problems actually arise during the time span of the OLRT evolution.

Problems that will be eliminated. The changes that are foreseen are discussed very briefly and in lay terms. In the group of problems that exists today, those that will be eliminated through adoption of an electronic system are:

1. The requirement to return checks to the drawer.
2. The extra handling required for certified and cashier's checks.
3. Stop payment responsibilities.
4. The requirement for presentation of an instrument for payment.
5. Kiting.
6. The difficulties created by forgeries and alteration.

The requirement to return checks to the drawer is one that has already outlived its usefulness, although it fulfills four demands at this time: Return is required by law in some areas; the canceled checks are used for reconciliation of the checking account; canceled checks provide proof of payment; and the return of the checks fills a psychological need of the drawer.

The direct legal requirement to return checks will be avoided, because checks will no longer be in existence. Reconciliation of accounts and proof of payment can be provided by periodic machine runs of all transactions for a given period. These machine runs, producing monthly statements, could be given the legal documentary status of canceled checks. Hence the statement would be a legal proof of payment which the individual could maintain for his personal records. Such runs would include the date of the transaction, the account identification of the payor and of the recipient, the amount paid, and the balance at completion of the run. This leaves only the psychological need of the drawer to see a piece of paper with his name on the front and the endorsement of the party he paid on the reverse. Bank of America is currently offering a service which provides its customers only a description, on the bank statement, of a deduction for payment of utility bills. It has met with little or no resistance. While this is an isolated experience, it provides the basis for a conclusion that very little customer education will be required to make a machine-run record of payment acceptable to the American public.

Certified checks and cashier's checks have two uses at this time. First, they are used to show that the party is capable of fulfilling a potential future obligation; that is, they are a substitute for a performance bond. Second, they are used to fulfill contractual requirements where such large sums of money change hands that the use of cash is not expedient, but positive proof that the payor has the funds is desired—for instance, in large real estate or commodity transactions.

In the first case, continuation of the use of certified or cashier's checks is foreseen; but in the second case, the transaction can be completed by the provision of a terminal device at the site of the transaction, and immediate proof of a transfer of funds can be established.

Stop payment capability will be nonexistent with the electronic transfer system. Instead, various forms of delays, such as short-term credit, will be used by the purchaser of an item to maintain his "cherished privilege." Reversal of the flow of funds to accommodate such requirements as return of a purchase will also be available, with such transactions made at the discretion of the party which originally received the funds.

Today's requirement for presentation of a check to receive payment will require modification; a series of digits, transmitted electronically, will be the check's equivalent. While the psychological effects may be a factor in this case, the legal precedents for recognition of electronic data processing output have already been established in court tests.

Kiting, or using the delay provided by check-processing time to afford false liquidity, will be eliminated, because processing will be instantaneous. Today's three-day processing cycles will be cut to seconds.

Forgeries and alterations will also be eliminated. Alterations could only be perpetrated by the operator of the terminal device, and any such attempt would be recognizable immediately. The only near equivalent of the forgery of today would be through theft and attempted use of the card identification device, and proper safeguards, as detailed earlier, will exclude that possibility.

Problems requiring changes in the law. A second group of problems will require for their solution either amplification or amendment of current laws. These problems include examination and audit requirements; limitations placed upon banks restricting the amount of capital which can be invested in data processing equipment; and restrictions placed upon banks, credit institutions, and retail outlets concerning disclosure of credit information.

Examination and audit laws will have to be expanded to include procedures for these functions in a totally electronic system. These requirements should be greatly simplified when standard programs are in use. The Federal Reserve has also recognized the importance of EDP in bank operations and has done much to train its personnel and revise its procedures to accommodate the change to EDP.

Banking laws now limit the percentage of capitalization which may be invested in electronic data processing centers. In the various stages of evolution, these limitations could seriously impede progress if the banks planned upon using their own resources for financing. Therefore, either external financing will have to be made available or the limiting laws will have to be relaxed. It is expected that recent activities of banks, in trying to expand their EDP facilities for present-day purposes, will influence early and favorable changes in these laws.

There are restrictions placed upon the amounts and kinds of credit information the different groups are allowed to furnish about their customers. These restrictions could make credit profiles less reliable than the profiles that would be possible if full disclosure were possible. As an OLRT credit information system has the potential for collecting and disseminating personal data more efficiently than present systems, there will eventually be a revised balance of pressures which seek, on the one hand, to centralize more information, and, on the other hand, to insure discriminating use of the information and the system. No serious legal problem is anticipated, however, since there is considerable room for improvement in credit information systems using only the information presently allowed.

Other legal implications. The Internal Revenue Service will have to accept proof of deductions from a machine run or a magnetic tape; the individual taxpayer will have ample proof of deductions recorded in the transaction files of the system without the necessity for receipt and record retention. (It is even possible that at some future date IRS will compute everyone's taxes and deduct them automatically.)

There are two other legal complications which could result from an electronic system such as has been detailed—antitrust implications and fair-trade problems.

The source of control for an integrated cash and credit system with its required equipment is discussed later on, but it will certainly be so expensive to install, to place into operation, and to operate that a parallel, duplicate system, or systems, most probably would not be feasible. This rules out competition and logically leads us to consideration of an authorized monopoly or integrated "computer utility." Government intervention in the form of rate setting, control of assets utilization, and so on, would, of course, be the logical next step.

Further, there will almost certainly be an effort made by the banks, and possibly by the retail institutions, to control the credit function. The possibility of this occurring will be related directly to the speed and force with which the credit bureaus apply themselves to establishing a place within the system and to the attitude of the antitrust division of the Attorney General's office toward such an action. No prognosis can be given except in the instance where the antitrust division refrains from acting and where the credit bureaus do nothing or too little. This instance would surely result in the credit bureaus' demise.

In the area of fair-trade practices, Government intervention will surely result unless utmost care is taken throughout the evolution to insure equity in establishing and applying the rate structure for data transmission, in accessing the computer, and in permitting purchases of the additional services made available by the system.

CONTROL AND OWNERSHIP OF THE ELECTRONIC CASH AND CREDIT SYSTEM

The question of who will own or control the nation's electronic cash and credit networks looms as one of the most important considerations for systems planners. Robert V. Head, formerly of Touche, Ross, Bailey & Smart, has discussed in a paper, "Emergence of the Checkless Society," the alternative economic sectors which will have a vested interest in the operation of the system. Much of what he said is incorporated in what follows.

Banks. Commercial bankers, as shown in earlier chapters, appear to be in the most logical position for developing cash and credit transfer systems capability; it is within the banking sector that the most advanced applications of OLRT systems for funds transfer are now to be found. Banks are clearly demonstrating the resources both for setting up the transfer mechanism and for supporting sufficient consumer loans to extend credit at the point of a retail transaction. Commercial bankers are regarding the electronic funds transfer systems as logical extensions of the other fiduciary services they are performing, and it is to be expected that banks will seek to maintain a strong hand in the control of the new systems.

Credit bureaus. Credit bureaus, seeking to meet the demands of their users for more rapid, comprehensive, and accurate data, are likely to offer OLRT services of their own with interface to merchants and banks, as has been discussed in earlier chapters. As an on-line participant in the system it is natural to expect that the credit bureaus will also be extremely interested in who controls and operates the system, to insure the protection of their own information files and of the clients whom they serve.

Retailers. The retail merchants in some areas may be unwilling to stand by idly while the system is introduced by some other economic sector. In fact, it is suggested by Mr. Head that retail merchants might band together in a community to set up credit transfer systems of their own, perhaps pooling accounts receivable as an evolutionary prelude to a full-funds transfer system. That the retailers might precede the bankers seems unlikely, but, in cases where this is so, it must be recognized that the system developers will be very reluctant to yield controlling authority to another group, such as the banks.

Hardware manufacturers. Equipment manufacturers might well view the emergence of funds transfer systems not only as an opportunity to supply substantial amounts of equipment but also as an opportunity to secure the substantial revenue that will accrue to whatever organization is successful in providing the service. The growth of OLRT service bureaus similar to the Key Data Corporation may well become organizational extensions of the manufacturers. If this becomes the case, it is possible that the manufacturers will emerge as a powerful element in the cash and credit economy of the future.

Communications companies. The communications common carrier companies, like the hardware manufacturers, might also contemplate a shift in their established role. Firms such as American Telephone and Telegraph and Western Union are already heavily involved with the development of computer-oriented data handling systems of all types. They could logically arrive at the conclusion that they would be willing not only to provide the needed data links and possibly the terminals but also to offer a full-scale service for electronic funds transfer. Even with overall control vested in another sector, it is clear that the communications common carriers will have a very large voice in control of the telecommunications aspects of the system in matters such as data transmission charges, transmission rates, and universal touch-tone network installation dates.

Finance companies. Some of the major finance companies presently have an advantage even over commercial banks in that many of their systems are already national in scope and are able to offer the universality so important to the funds transfer mechanism. The existence of a well-established national organization, added to the finance companies' capability to provide consumer credit, places these institutions in an excellent position to establish and control their own funds transfer systems. Like the retail merchants, if this sector becomes the initiator, it will not be inclined to yield controlling power to other organizations. Though such a development is possible, it does seem unlikely at this date that the finance companies will be the initiators of a major OLRT network for transferring funds and credit to facilitate retail shopping.

Independents. Independent entrepreneurs with vision and substantial capital backing could well be the first to launch electronic cash and credit systems in communities where the established organizations, in particular the banks, fail to move aggressively to exploit the opportunities inherent in the OLRT transfer networks. The controlling power of any such entrepreneurs would be substantial—equivalent, say, to the power of a local bank in terms of credit-line extension and the like.

Government. The Federal Government will inevitably have a strong controlling influence in the system, regardless of who has primary control at local levels, because of the far-reaching implications of such a system for various Government agencies. However, there is no assurance that the Government's concern will be limited to regulation of the way in which these systems evolve and operate. It is altogether conceivable that the Federal Government may be compelled to become the owner and operator of these systems as well. The Government's participation in the Federal Reserve System, in check processing, and in the postal system indicates clearly that the Government's present involvement in funds transfer is substantial and that it could be developed considerably further.

From what has been said, it is clear that in the first years, at least, we can expect no uniform pattern of control to emerge. Problems of interface, compatibility, and systems redundancy, to name a few, will resolve overtime into both standardization of components and the emergence of the best systems and most capable operators. As already suggested, we believe that banks as a group will emerge as the primary initiator and controller of future systems, with a strong regulatory influence from the Federal Government; an ownership and control structure similar to COMSAT, with joint Government and private-sector participation, may very well be the ultimate outcome, as suggested by many who have examined this problem. The alternatives to allowing the Government to have a substantial amount of participation could allow the business of credit information and funds transfer to fall to a very large national corporation, with all the resulting consequences of monopoly control. The resolution of the control and ownership questions will become increasingly complex as more and more organizations perceive opportunities to become part of the system; this aspect of the checkless society will undoubtedly draw increasing amounts of attention and concern in the years immediately ahead and warrants careful study by those venturing to establish their own position in what is to come.

THE IMPLICATIONS FOR THE FEDERAL GOVERNMENT

Robert Head identifies a list of at least 12 Federal agencies that will need to be intimately concerned with the emergence of the electronic cash and credit system because of the effect the system will have on each of their activities. The two most obvious are the Treasury Department and the Federal Reserve System.

The Treasury. Within the Treasury Department, the Office of Comptroller of the Currency has control over Federal bank regulations. As discussed in the earlier chapter on legal problems, many accommodations in current bank regulations will be called for as large funds-transfer networks are established. The Internal Revenue Service will be concerned for many reasons, including revenue forecasting and collection as well as taxpayer identification. The electronic system will also require smaller amounts of currency and coin in circulation, directly affecting the planning and operations of the Bureau of Engraving and Printing and of the U.S. Mint.

The Federal Reserve. The Federal Reserve System, responsible for establishing credit regulations, operating interbank data communications, and processing check transfers, will be dramatically affected by the envisioned system. On February 9, 1966, George Mitchell, a member of the board of governors of the Federal Reserve System, delivered a paper on the potential impact of electronic funds transfer systems on the Federal Reserve System and on Federal Reserve float. Mr. Mitchell states that EDP and wire transmission technology has already begun to reduce Federal Reserve float and will, in the foreseeable future, eliminate it. ("Float" is the aggregate dollar amount of checks on any given day for which credit has been passed by Federal Reserve banks and branches to their depositing member banks without receipt of payment from drawee banks, less the amount of such items, if any, for which payment has been received but credit not yet given.) During 1965 the average daily amount of Federal Reserve float outstanding was $1.8 billion, amounting to a huge extension of free credit to banks and depositors. In the same year the Federal Reserve banks and branches handled over five billion checks and other cash items having an average daily value in excess of $7 billion.

This huge amount of float has been kept in check only through the installation of MICR and EDP technologies, which allow checks to be processed through the Federal Reserve System at the rate of some 60,000 per hour versus a previous 1,500 per hour.

Wire transmission technology is now suggesting further reductions in, if not the total elimination of, float through one of two processes, both of which are currently under study by the Federal Reserve System. The first, a near-range program, would call for the immediate crediting via communications networks to the reserve account of the depositing bank of all checks deposited for collection in Federal Reserve banks and branches, with a simultaneous charging to the reserve account or correspondent account of the drawee bank.

The second process involves a longer-range prospect and is the system of cash and credit transfer proposed by the authors, which would eliminate the use of the check itself for the bulk of regular money settlements. In the checkless society as explained earlier, the payor initiates the settlement process by communicating, not with the payee in the form of a check, but with his own bank, notifying it directly whom to pay and how much. This concept, when applied to transactions which pass through the Federal Reserve System, eliminates both checks and float.

Mr. Mitchell suggests that the process of instantaneous settlement and deposit accounting for funds transfers between banks and for bank deposits could be carried out by between 250 or so computer centers located throughout the country.

The structural and organizational changes in the Federal Reserve System to accommodate such a completely new system are staggering. However, the possibility of eliminating the $1.8 billion in daily float provides a major incentive for the Federal Reserve System to develop an electronic cash transfer as soon as possible. Float is also subject to widely fluctuating volume levels from day to day, because of snowstorms, floods, and other conditions. These fluctuations present serious operating problems to the Federal Open Market Committee in its attempt to maintain bank reserve positions at agreed-upon levels. Surely, any technological developments which will assist the elimination of this problem would merit close study by the monetary authorities.

Other agencies. Some of the other Government agencies suggested in Head's paper which will be affected by an electronic cash and credit system (perhaps to a lesser degree than the Treasury and the Federal Reserve System) include the following:

The Bureau of the Budget, with its national budgetary planning responsibilities, will recognize considerable shifts in the levels of consumer credit and other affected variables which may require modification of economic reporting and planning procedures.

The Federal Communications Commission will be heavily involved in the data transmission requirements of the proposed system, both as a regulatory agent and as policy-forming body.

The Council of Economic Advisers will surely be interested and concerned with the overall economic implications of the new system.

The Department of Labor will have to monitor the employment implications of job displacement and new-job creation and may even become involved in manpower planning for the system.

The Department of Health, Education and Welfare should be interested in the system's effect on the individual, not to mention the possibility of making automatic welfare payments through the system.

The Federal Deposit Insurance Corporation will be concerned with the effect the new financial system will have on individual bank balances and levels of bank credit.

The Department of Justice, Antitrust Division, will naturally be caught up with the antitrust considerations. The Federal Bureau of Investigation will likely be interested in the means of customer identification and interstate law enforcement.

The Department of State might well be interested in the implications of a worldwide complex of automatic funds transfer systems.

The Post Office Department will be interested in the impact of decreasing amounts of business and consumer mail and the resultant effect on postal revenues. The complete obsolescence of the postal money order might be implied.

Thus the effect of electronic cash and credit systems upon our national economy has to be evaluated carefully by many agencies. It is clear that the checkless society will affect many more institutions than just the commercial banks.

SOCIAL IMPLICATIONS

Of all the complex adjustments which will have to be made before an electronic cash and credit system can become fully operational, some of the most difficult changes must occur in the areas of human behavior, attitudes, and work patterns. The common element of all the problems to be discussed is the problem of change itself: Unless there is a distinctive "gain" involved in the replacement of a habitual pattern of activity with a new one, individuals and groups are naturally reluctant to make the change. When other specific sources of resistance, such as regional parochialism, fear of direct competition from new or different types of economic units, or fear of anything new, are combined with the general resistance to change, the process of winning acceptance for the proposed transfer system may be very difficult indeed. The major areas where these problems will occur are as follows:

1. The manning and operation of the system.
2. The reactions of individuals to the new method of making transactions.
3. The resistance of several groups of businesses on economic grounds.
4. The impending threat of "big brotherism."

Manning the system. Finding, training, and maintaining qualified people to operate the system will be no easy task. There are already serious short-ages of critical-skill workers in the occupations related to computer activities, such as systems analysts, programmers, even key-punch operators. Although the hardware manufacturers, the larger firms using computers, and the privately operated schools are attempting to train large numbers of people for these jobs, supply is still running far behind demand.

A significant increase in demand for computer technicians can be expected when banks, credit bureaus, and retailers plan electronic cash and credit systems, not simply because the programming involved is complex but because identical programming tasks will probably be duplicated many times in sort of hodgepodge development of regional centers. Even if the hardware manufacturers develop general-purpose programs to control cash and credit transfers (as they have for other applications), each center will still have to adapt the program to its own unique application requirements demanding the time of technicians skilled in computer operations.

Within each regional center, the programming required to tie each unit into the central switching computer will require thousands of man-hours of work. Competing businesses within a region, such as two banks tied to the same central switcher, are not likely to share programs; even today bankers frequently view their "own" programs as superior to functionally identical programs used by competitors. It's all part of the competitive spirit, perhaps. Competitive aspects of computer utilization (and the corresponding cost of redundant programming and systems work) will likely become more pronounced before it gets better as units within the system each hasten to be the first to develop and offer new types of computer-based services to utilize their OLRT capability.

The shortage of technicians, which may continue far into the future, will require more than the basic economic mechanism of supply and demand to provide a solution. The problems of educating young people as to the importance of the computer's existence, of impressing upon older people the need for continually upgrading their skills, and of encouraging the unskilled to seek opportunities in new industries or areas will all become so urgent that increased Government activity can be expected to help change basic attitudes and provide training.

A more subtle aspect of the same problem, which cannot be solved by Government-sponsored training programs or Government-granted economic incentives, is the difficult task of updating management's skills in computer usage. It will not be possible for the electronic cash and credit system to get off the ground until those managers responsible for making the required investments are also capable of using the system effectively. This implies that managers will need to develop both increasingly higher levels of sophistication regarding computers and also more detailed technical knowledge in terms of managing the computing operation.

Reactions to the new system. Three problems relating to individuals' present transaction habits may impede customer acceptance of electronic funds transfers. With the checking system, customers have the ability to stop payment on a check if they are dissatisfied with the merchandise they purchased. This customer expectation cannot easily be reconciled by the proposed system. What could be done technically, however, would be to include a system feature permitting a type of payment delay. Purchasers of relatively expensive items could delay actual payment for a specified period (at which time the demand deposit transfer would take place automatically) in exchange for payment of a flat or percentage-based "interest" fee. Since the number of stop-payments is not significant in relation to the number of *transactions,* the social resistance to loss of the privilege could easily be overcome by an educational campaign to inform customers of such optional methods of withholding or delaying payment.

A second problem which has attracted the attention of pessimistic students of American social behavior is that of the possibility of a "credit spree" occasioned by the sudden ease with which individuals could spend up to the limits of their lines of credit under the proposed system. While the recent dramatic increases in consumer credit have been viewed by some as an indication of a lack of financial responsibility (even the degeneration of moral values), it does not appear that the increased convenience of using an identification card versus writing a check or arranging for credit at a store is so great as to cause a revolutionary shift in credit-purchasing habits.

Another potential problem will be reactions to the loss of check float which all present users of checks will experience. The time lag between the writing of a check and the actual deduction of that amount from one's checking account balance has been used to advantage by groups ranging from students, whose checking account balances may ride perilously close to zero, to huge corporations, which use the time value of money to make more money. While the effect of the elimination of float may be mitigated in the case of businesses, whose present check transactions take place both ways, those individuals who could not maintain positive account balances if all outstanding checks were suddenly posted, will be forced to revise their purchasing and payment habits or pay the interest charges on short-term extensions of overdraft credit. While this may be of concern to experienced practitioners of the art (kiters most notably), it is felt that the general public, including those who are not aware of the time involved in processing a check, will be able to forgo the benefits of float in exchange for the extra convenience of instantaneous transactions and possibly the elimination or reduction of charges for checks and account servicing. Many people never even consider the concept of float anyway and *assume* that checks they write are instantaneously deducted from their account.

Business resistance. Managers of smaller banks and retail stores have voiced the fear that the installation of an electronic cash and credit system will cost them their identity—that they will be "swallowed up" by the larger units within the system. Smaller banks which cannot afford large computer installations have worried that the control of the electronic system might rest entirely with the large banks; also, since frequent personal contact with depositors will decrease once deposits and withdrawals can be made from remote locations, the controlling banks would be able to out-market smaller banks by offering exclusive services. Actually, the large banks will need to enlist the joint participation of the small banks in order to eliminate the need for processing the checks written by small-bank customers; if only part of the banks and stores in a market area convert to an electronic system, the problem of maintaining duplicate check-processing and electronic-processing facilities mitigates the electronic system's advantages. One of the beauties of OLRT technology is that small banks will be able to market all the computer-based services that the large banks will offer, by sharing computer time with the larger banks or by joint ventures of smaller banks, *without* a disproportionate investment in computers and equipment.

A previous chapter has discussed the fact that many retailers fear the elimination of their own credit-granting facilities will be a loss of an important marketing tool. They claim their present credit cards provide an exclusivity that is worth more than the cost of operating their credit-granting services, that their credit standards are more liberal than the banks' and therefore attract customers who would not receive credit elsewhere, and that the loss of credit-granting capability would actually cost some of the large efficient retailers the profit they make on credit operations. A more general concern with retailers is that they have not yet had sufficient years of computer experience to appreciate fully all advantages of the OLRT system. Many retailers are still busy resisting the basic concept of computerization and using computers to help in their internal operations.

Most of these fears can be allayed by demonstrating to the retailers the economic gains which will be available to OLRT retailer systems participants as developed in Chapter VI.

Big brother. The last, most serious social problem which the new system raises is the question of control not only of the system but of people. We have seen in preceding chapters that there are viable, convincing arguments to be made for integrating the functions of banking, retailing, and credit through electronic networks. One of the natural results (and advantages) of doing this would be to consolidate the information about individuals and thereby broaden information "coverage." But unless the development of proper controls over this potentially huge source of personal information precedes or accompanies the building of the system itself, confusion over the authority to use information will undoubtedly result; and possibilities for unscrupulous use of data might arise.

Even if we assume that the security safeguards in existence now can be kept intact and that improper commercial use of information will be impossible, there still remains the question of possible governmental use of the collected personal data. It is conceivable, for example, that deterministic applications of governmental standards could affect opportunities for individuals to qualify for government or civilian jobs, hold elective or appointive office, or enter advanced publicly owned schools. It is possible, of course, to conjure up an Orwellian world of complete governmental surveillance and control, all made possible by what started out to be an efficient way of transacting business!

The authors do not believe, however, that we need have any deterring fears of 1984 when we consider the automated system proposed. In the first place, the individual's right to privacy has historically been of such importance to the makers and interpreters of law that the present restrictions upon usage of personal information will never be relaxed, nor will the system of checks and balances which controls the relative power of interested governmental groups ever change to the extent that one group or agency could dominate control of the system. The other, more basic reason, is that the information that would be available within the proposed system is exactly the same information that is being collected now. All this information *could* be gathered (most of it legally) by anyone or any agency *today* that wanted to do so.

The internal reorganization of banks' files to build central information files, the development of computerized credit files, and the establishment of customer files in retail organizations have not triggered a rash of speculation that "big brother" is upon us. The authors can foresee, therefore, no reason for believing that the simple connection of these files through on-line data links will do so either.

CHAPTER IX

TIMETABLE FOR ACTION •

IN 1967-1968 THE CONCEPT of on-line, real-time systems will be adapted to the savings account operations of many large banks and to the credit files of almost all the country's large credit bureaus. A large number of department stores will experiment with computerized cash register systems which will update inventory records, provide sales analyses, and automate credit transactions; at least some of these systems will operate in real-time. Almost all supermarket chains will have computerized inventory control and order processing, and many chains will have automated check-cashing approvals. Pioneering banks will greatly expand the scope of their computer-based customer services and will experiment with OLRT links to selected retail stores and credit bureaus. Automatic wage payment and utility bill collection will become common. Alternative universal numbering schemes will be investigated. Progressive banks will work hard to perfect the systems design for central information files.

1970. Most banks will have developed central information files on their depositors which will be stored in random-access, third-generation computer-based systems. Credit-scoring procedures will be standardized and automated in most credit bureaus. Many small, local bureaus will have been absorbed by banks. Most large banks will issue credit cards, either developed by themselves or by acquisition of existing independent organizations. A multiplicity of reciprocal arrangements, whereby one bank's card is recognized by another bank or store for check-cashing or credit privileges, will be established. Most bank cards will be based on the client's social security number. Many on-line, real-time links between stores, credit bureaus, and banks will be in local use. Bank-by-phone devices will be available in many areas on a "pioneering" basis.

1975. Entire metropolitan areas will be tied together by means of electronic cash and credit systems. These areas will be ones in which the most favorable combination of circumstances exists: a fully installed touch-tone line system, a progressive bank or group of banks, forward-looking retailers, and a large, dominant credit bureau. Other regional areas will all have some elements of the system in full operation. No new credit cards will be issued by individual banks. Rather, identification cards (all conforming to a national format and numbering system) will be issued, with the name of the customer's bank imprinted upon each for promotional purposes only. Total check volume will be dramatically reduced; many banks will discontinue their own check plans. Federal Reserve float will be eliminated; checks which are processed through the Fed will be handled through facsimile transmission or simply by an electronic funds transfer system which collects, through a wire transfer network, check items to be transferred, with the physical check forwarded on to the paying bank later as time permits.

GLOSSARY

audit trail—a historical, traceable record of transactions processed through the system.

batch processing—the processing of blocks of data, in sequential order and as a discrete job or batch.

buffer—a storage device used to compensate for a difference in rate of flow of data, or time of occurrence of events, when transmitting data from one device to another.

central information file (CIF)—a computerized device for storing and cross-referencing the information pertaining to a customer's accounts.

central switching computer (CSC)—an electronic switching device linking all the system participants within a region, used for the purpose of routing the information being transmitted between on-line participants.

central transmission unit (CTU)—See **multiplexor**.

computer credit file (CCF)—a central information file specifically serving a credit information bureau.

credit scoring—application of statistical techniques for more objectively and scientifically evaluating the credit-worthiness of an applicant.

disc memory—magnetic disc. A flat circular plate with a magnetic surface on which data can be stored by selective magnetization of portions of the flat surface.

facsimile transmission—the electronic transmission of a picture, fingerprint, document, or other image from one location to another.

funds identification card—a machine-readable card which identifies the customer to the OLRT funds transfer system.

hard copy—a physical document, such as a sales receipt or canceled check, to show proof of transaction.

hardware—mechanical or electronic components of the computing system.

multiplexor—a device for interleaving or permitting simultaneous transmission of two or more messages on a single channel.

on-line, real-time (OLRT)—a computerized network of hardware devices in a configuration permitting direct communication from remote terminal stations to central computer files with the specific capacity of servicing funds transactions and information inquiries within very rapid, "tolerable" limits of elapsed time.

135

post giro—a funds transfer network operated through a postal system specifically requiring that funds to be transferred be placed with the transferring agent who then places the funds with the payee.

random access—a file storage system, permitting the computerized retrieval of single records without requiring a sequential searching of the entire file from the beginning.

software—the systems and programming instructions required to operate the on-line computer devices.

terminal device—an instrument which reads the funds identification card, establishes electronic connections with the rest of the OLRT network, and relays other variable data to and from the point of input.

touch-tone telephone—a telephonic instrument which uses push buttons in place of the regular dial device, and which transmits "dialed-in" digital data by altering the frequency or pitch of transmitted pulses, rather than by transmitting single frequency, Morse-code-like pulses.

voice-print—a technique of recording in computer memory a digital representation of an individual's unique voice pattern.

BIBLIOGRAPHY

BOOKS AND PERIODICALS

Allen, S. P., "Credit Card Operation That Has Hit the Jackpot," *Burroughs' Clearing House,* September 1, 1964.

American Bankers Association, *Proceedings,* National Automation Conference, 1964.

————, *Proceedings,* National Automation Conference, 1965.

Auburn, H. W. (ed.), *Comparative Banking,* Waterlow & Sons, Ltd., 1960.

Barryman, J. T., "Commercial Bank Goes Real Time," *Datamation,* July 1965.

Bazelon, David T., *The Paper Economy,* Random House, Inc., 1959.

Belcher, David W., "The How and Why of Retail Credit," *University of Illinois Bulletin,* 1950.

Brennan, E. J., Jr., "Another Look at Charge Account Banking," *The Credit World,* November 1965.

"C and A Capital Report," *Computers and Automation,* July 1965.

"Charge Accounts at the Chase," *Business Week,* October 25, 1958.

"Charge It Plan That Really Took Off," *Business Week,* February 27, 1965.

"Data Collection and Accumulation," *Automation,* January 1963.

Davenport, W. P., "Touch Tone," *Data Processing,* October 1965.

Dearden, John, "Management Information Systems," case material for Harvard Business School, copyright President and Fellows of Harvard College, 1965.

Driver, Albert W., Jr., "Retail Revolving Credit and the Usury Statutes," *Quarterly Report.*

Duncan, Delbert J., and Charles F. Phillips, *Retailing: Principles and Methods,* Richard D. Irwin, Inc., 1963.

"EDP in State and Local Governments at Mid-Decade," *Automatic Data Processing Newsletter,* May 10, 1965.

Federal Deposit Insurance Corporation, *Annual Report,* Table 16, p. 78.

Federal Reserve Bank of Boston, "Performance Characteristics of High Earning Banks," 1964, p. 1.

"FNCB" (used for earning figure on commercial banks last five years), *Fortune.*

Goll, T., "Criminal World Faces Duel with Computer," *Los Angeles Times,* July 11, 1965.

Goshay, Robert C., *Information Technology in the Insurance Industry,* Richard D. Irwin, Inc., 1964.

Greenberger, Martin, "Banking and the Information Utility," address before the American Bankers Association Automation Conference, March 9, 1965.

————, "Decline and Fall of the Check," *The Bankers Magazine.*

Head, Robert V., *Automatic Credit Transfer Systems: Emergence of the Checkless Society,* 1965.

————, "The Checkless Society," *Datamation,* March 1966.

Hooker, W. G. (ed), *Computerizing the Credit—Accounts Receivable Operation,* National Retail Merchants Association, 1965.

"Installment Loans—How Profitable?" *New England Business Review,* February 1962.

Jordan, Harry, President, Credit Data Corporation, address before the National Installment Credit Conference, April 4, 1966.

Joseph, Allen B., *Methods of Evaluating Retail Information Systems,* National Retail Merchants Association, 1964.

Klock, Charles G., "Credit Risk Selection Through Statistical Evaluation," *Credit Management Year Book 1965/66,* National Retail Merchants Association, 1965.

————, "Credit Currents," pilot study for General Electric Credit Corp., February 1965.

Lockheed Missiles & Space Co., final report to California Statewide Information System Study, July 30, 1965.

"Mechanical Voice Now Answers Inquiries," *Auditgram,* November 1965.

Mitchell, George W., statement before the Legal and Monetary Affairs Subcommittee of the Committee on Government Operations, House of Representatives, February 9, 1966.

"More Areas of Standardization Needed for Best Use of New Bank Technology," *American Banker,* November 8, 1965.

Mosher, Richard N., "Credit Risk Selection Through Statistical Evaluation," *Credit Management Year Book, 1965/66,* National Retail Merchants Association, 1965.

NABAC (The Association for Bank Audit, Control and Operation), *Data Transmission in Banking,* NABAC, 1965.

————, *Directory of Bank Automation,* NABAC, 1966.

National Association of Credit Management Survey on Credit Reporting Industry, 1964.

National Credit Association, *Retail Credit Management,* McGraw-Hill Book Co., Inc., 1963.

National Retail Merchants Association, *Credit Management Year Book 1965/66,* NRMA, 1965.

————, "Departmental Merchandising and Operating Results," Controllers Congress, NRMA, 1965.

"New Shuffle in Credit Cards," *Business Week,* November 3, 1962.

"Next in Banking: Pay Bills by Phone," *Business Week,* November 13, 1965.

Nikolaieff, George A., "Bank in the Billfold," *The Wall Street Journal,* December 1965.

"One Number to a Customer," *American Banker,* October 28, 1965.

Patterson, Harlan R., "A Study of the Market Served by Bank Charge Plans," *Credit World,* October 1964.

———, "What Spells Success for Bank Charge Plans," *Banking,* February 1964.

Peterson, C. P., and others, "Worldwide Report on Banking," address before the American Bankers Association Automation Conference.

Reistad, Dale L., "Banking Automation—1975," *Banking,* July, October, November 1964.

———, "Dear Mr. Bank President," *Datamation,* July 1965.

———, "What Telecommunications Will Do for Banking," *Investment Dealers' Digest,* October 18, 1965.

Report of the Royal Commission on Banking and Finance, 1964, Queen's Printer, Canada, 1964.

Ridgeway, F., "Pure Oil Using Local Bank's Credit Cards," *National Petroleum News,* February 1965.

Schnee, Donald R., and Walter E. Trabbold, "Progress in Information Systems," *Bank of Delaware.*

"Scientific and Business Users Close the Computer Look," *Control Engineering.*

"Small Cities and Time Sharing," *Public Automation,* June 1965.

Sprague, Richard E., *Electronic Business Systems,* The Ronald Press Company, 1962.

———, "Information Utilities," *Financial Executive,* October 1965.

Spindeltop, Inc., "Preliminary Analysis of Electronic Payment and Credit Systems," 1965.

Thomson, F. P., *Giro Credit Transfer Systems,* Porgama Press and Macmillan, 1964.

"Throwing in the Sponge: Chase Manhattan Bank Is Abandoning Its Credit Card Dream," *Forbes,* February 1, 1962.

Touche, Ross, Bailey & Smart, "Evaluation of IBM Study for Automation of Greater Houston," 1964.

———, "New York Retail Credit Bureaus Survey for Teleregister Corporation," June 3, 1964.

———, "Study of Customer Credit Costs on Department Stores, 1963," National Retail Merchants Association, 1964.

———, "A System for Automatic Value Exchange," March 1966.

Trabbold, Walter E., address before National Association of Mutual Savings Banks.

Trotta, L. A., *Facts You Should Know About Revolving Credit, Installment Credit, and Credit Legislation,* National Retail Merchants Association, 1964.

Uniform Commercial Code Handbook, Ad Press Ltd., 1964.

U.S. Board of Governors, Federal Reserve System, "Chartbook on Financial and Business Statistics."

————, "Supplement to Banking and Monetary Statistics," Section 9, December 1965.

U.S. Department of Commerce, Bureau of Census, Statistical Abstract, "Changes in a Class of Operating Branch Offices," #606, 1965.

————, "Consumer Credit," #635, 1965.

————, "Consumer Installment Credit Outstanding," #636, 1965.

————, "Demand Deposit Accounts," #605, 1965.

Weiss, E. B., "Will Banks Become Merchandise Retailers?" *Advertising Age,* August 6, 1962.

Zaegel, Richard J., "Numerical Scoring as an Aid to Credit Granting," *Credit Currents,* March 1964.

Zimmerman, William, "Computer Leaves the Luxury Class; Becomes Necessity for U.S. Banks," *American Banker,* January-March 1966.

Zipp, A. R., "A Practical View of Universal Credit," *Datamation,* March 1966.

PAMPHLETS AND BROCHURES

Account Numbering Systems, Burroughs Corporation.

Advanced Business Systems Newsletter, Touche, Ross, Bailey & Smart.

Bank Central Information System Locate File, International Business Machine Co., Ltd.

Bank Central Information System on the IBM System 360, International Business Machine Co., Ltd.

Banking by Phone, Bell Systems.

Burroughs On-Line Teller System, Burroughs Corporation.

Central Information System at the Bank of Delaware, International Business Machine Co., Ltd.

Credit Bureau Operations on the IBM 360, International Business Machine Co., Inc.

Customer Information File for Banks, Design Guide, International Business Machine Co., Ltd.

Data Communications Concept, International Business Machine Co., Ltd.

Datanet 30, General Electric Co.

Datanet 30, Implementation of a Switching Center, General Electric Co.

Datanet 760 System for Customer Service Applications, General Electric Co.

Demand Deposit Accounting, Honeywell, Incorporated.

Disk Storage Concepts, International Business Machine Co., Ltd.

GE/Dartmouth Time Sharing System, General Electric Co.

IBM System 360 Demand Deposits, International Business Machine Co., Ltd.

Impact of Time Sharing On Data Processing Management, General Electric Co.

Instant Access Data Communications System, Burroughs Corporation.

Managing Banks in a Changing Economy, Touche, Ross, Bailey & Smart.

Minutes of X3.8 Task Force on Individual and Business Identification, February 9, 1966.

Modular Random Access Memory, Burroughs Corporation.

Monetary Institution Data Automation System, Control Data Corp.

New Concept in Computer Time Sharing, General Electric Co.

New Generation Computing Power for Banks, Honeywell, Incorporated.

On-Line Savings with the Compatible 1400, General Electric Co.

Progress in Information Systems, Bank of Delaware.

Savings Accounting, Burroughs Corporation

Teleprocessing Equipment, International Business Machine Co., Ltd.

Teller Unit Monitoring Program for On-Line Banking Systems, Honeywell, Incorporated.

Time-Sharing System Manual, General Electric Co.

COMPANIES AND ASSOCIATIONS THAT COOPERATED IN THE AUTHORS' RESEARCH

American Bankers Association

American Telephone and Telegraph Company

Banco Popular de Puerto Rico

Bank of America

Bank of Delaware

Bank of Montreal

Booz, Allen and Hamilton, Inc.

Charge Account Bankers Association

Computer Control Company

Control Data Corporation

Credit Lyonnais, Paris

DASA Corporation

Federal Reserve Bank of Boston

Federal Reserve Bank of New York

First National Bank of Boston

First National Bank of Seattle

First National City Bank

General Electric Company

General Telephone and Electronics Corporation

Harvard Computer Center

Harvard Graduate School of Business Administration

Honeywell, Incorporated

International Business Machines Corporation

Jordan Marsh Company

Key Data Corporation

LeFebure, Incorporated

Microwave Associates, Inc.

NABAC, The Association for Bank Audit, Control and Operation

National Retail Merchants Association

New York State Bankers Association

Pilgrim Plastics Company

Project MAC, Massachusetts Institute of Technology

Rand Corporation

Sperry Utah

Storm Shoes

Sveriges Kreditbank, Stockholm, Sweden

Touche, Ross, Bailey & Smart

U.S. Department of Commerce, Boston, Mass.